KU-503-219

FINDING ROMAN BRITAIN

By the same author:

The Young Archaeologist's Handbook (with Lloyd Laing)
All About Archaeology (with Lloyd Laing)

FINDING ROMAN BRITAIN

Jennifer Laing

DAVID & CHARLES

NEWTON ABBOT   LONDON   NORTH POMFRET (VT)   VANCOUVER

HERTFORDSHIRE
COUNTY LIBRARY
J
J936.2
8693244

ISBN 0 7153 7406 0

Library of Congress Catalog Card Number: 77–89368

© Jennifer Laing 1977

All rights reserved. No part of this
publication may be reproduced, stored
in a retrieval system, or transmitted,
in any form or by any means, electronic,
mechanical, photocopying, recording or
otherwise, without the prior permission
of David & Charles (Publishers) Limited

Set in 11 on 13pt Linotype Baskerville
and printed in Great Britain
by Latimer Trend & Company Ltd Plymouth
for David & Charles (Publishers) Limited
Brunel House   Newton Abbot   Devon

Published in the United States of America
by David & Charles Inc
North Pomfret   Vermont 05053   USA

Published in Canada
by Douglas David & Charles Limited
1875 Welch Street   North Vancouver   BC

Contents

Introduction

It was a misty spring morning when I arrived at the village of Lympne in Kent for the first time. I was armed with a list of eight not-to-be-missed Roman sites, and the enthusiasm of a very new student who has borrowed the family car for a spot of field-work. I drove round the village a couple of times looking for the Roman fort, and saw only a notice to Stutfall Castle. Assuming this to be some crenellated medieval ruin, and determined not to be side-tracked, I ignored the signpost.

Eventually, unwilling to lose face by asking the help of a local inhabitant on what must surely be a simple problem for a serious romanist, I consulted the official guide to the area. Apparently the best place to view the fort was not from close at hand but from the scarp above. With a new objective, I found what seemed to be the right place and set off down a muddy path. Gazing out over the Romney Marshes, I noticed the sudden change in gradient where the sea had once lapped inland, the telltale flatness of the fields where salt water had once supported the bobbing fleet. This landscape would once have rung with the cries of the unit of Tungrian sailors from Gaul who were based at Portus Lemanis (Lympne). It all seemed very remote and evocative of another age, but no ancient walls greeted my eyes. No doubt they were there, but I failed to recognise them. Roman remains of astonishing magnitude have a disconcerting way of blending into their surroundings. It was some weeks later that I discovered that Stutfall Castle, the alleged and maligned 'medieval' stronghold was the Roman fort itself. The seeker of Roman Britain must be prepared for such red herrings.

It was a further nine years before fate decreed that I should visit that corner of the Romney Marshes again. The desolation and the massive fallen walls were not a disappointment. Nor, however, were they informative. The stones themselves appear to tell little about why troops built walls fourteen feet thick and over twenty-five feet high into a huge pentagon, or why the fort was abandoned. In fact it belongs to the third century, a period when the Roman Empire was politically unstable. The garrison at Lympne had to be ready to defend the shores against all-comers. The garrison would have heard of depositions and assassinations, bids for power, massive military coups and spectacular failures. In that century alone over thirty emperors were raised to the purple. The modern observer, however, might be forgiven for gleaning no more information than did the antiquary William Stukeley, who described the fort as 'so broken that it is as if Time was in a merry humour and ruined it in sport'.

Yet it is the very stones and their surroundings that through excavation and fieldwork reveal stories of human passions that well surpass the content of modern thrillers. From such research we learn details of Romano-British life that would have astonished the Romans themselves.

The Romans turn up in unexpected places. The grey-black Anglo-Saxon church at Escomb, County Durham, is a tall narrow gem of primitive architecture that has withstood the northern climate for over 1,200 years. The most incongruous features, to the architectural historian, are the five windows inserted in a phase of modernisation in the Middle Ages. But further surprises lurk in the external north wall of the nave. Here is a finely-dressed stone with the inverted and mysterious inscription VI LEG. This is not some beautifully executed graffito, perilously carved by some ancient miscreant, but the indisputable work of soldiers of the Sixth Legion intent on the more desperate business of bringing the province of Britannia into the civilised world. The stone, and possibly part of the chancel arch, was almost certainly brought from the nearest ruined fort and re-used by the Saxon architects.

In the stories of medieval minstrels, too, lie half-remembered events that once shattered the western world. 'Maxen Wledig was emperor of Rome, and a comelier and a better and a wiser man that any that came before him', explains the writer of one of the stories in the *Mabinogion*, a collection of Welsh folk tales set down in the twelfth century. Behind these simple lines lies a story of courage and ambition that had been handed down for centuries. The Spanish-born commander of Roman Britain, Magnus Maximus, frustrated by slow promotion, took advantage of the unpopularity of the emperor and decided to seize the Western Provinces for himself. In AD 383, with the eloquence and leadership of many a general before and after him, he persuaded the legions, and probably as many volunteers, to join his cause. Crossing the Channel, he proclaimed himself emperor. The bid was successful and he ruled for five years until his death at the hand of the new and rightful emperor Theodosius. His popularity did not die with him. When the Romans finally dissociated themselves from the province of Britannia in about AD 410, the kingdoms that grew up paid tribute to the man who had challenged the greatest military force of the time and had so nearly won. Several Welsh and one Scottish king-lists trace their foundations back to Maxen Wledig (Magnus Maximus).

The Romans came to Britain permanently in AD 43 and during the following 367 years transformed the island. If it took them 20,000 legionaries (about a fifth or sixth of their entire numbers) and as many auxiliaries, they left indelible marks on the landscape, the technology and above all the minds of the Britons.

Immediately the province became independent, people began a quest for Britannia that has led inexorably to the present studies in pottery and placenames, metalwork and masonry, and to the modern excavations. Faced with a dearth of instructions from Rome, with unsafe trade routes, wasted cornfields, dead industries and unemployment, the Romano–British valiantly sought to maintain the Roman way of life. They stoked the central heating units and swept the city streets long after it was safe to ride from Carlisle to Chester. Many had peaceful relationships with the Anglo-Saxon, Pictish or Irish settlers, but others fought on with a desperation that has been immortalised in legend. The mythical King Arthur would have repelled his Saxon enemies from a hill stronghold that boasted not merely outdated ramparts but a Roman-style gateway and palisade. In the four centuries of Roman rule, the southern areas of Britain at least had become Roman.

By the seventh century the Anglo-Saxons prevailed as the dominant force, and the Britons were absorbed into the new kingdoms. The few glimmering memories that might have remained of the province of Britannia were rekindled in 597 when St Augustine landed in Kent. This was the second army of Rome—this time bringing not civilisation but Christianity to the pagan Saxons. Roman vestments were worn and a standard based on those carried by the legion was borne. Stone churches were built on Roman lines, often on ruined fort sites, and from the very stonework first hewn by Roman soldiers. The Saxon kingdoms were introduced to the ways of civilisation and Christianity. They acquired a taste for things classical that was later manifested in the superb schools of British manuscript illumination.

In 1066 the Normans invaded England and introduced, amongst other classically-based phenomena, architecture derived from the Roman. Latin was kept alive in ecclesiastical and educated circles throughout the Middle Ages, but it was not until a more subtle invasion from Italy in the Renaissance that Rome was focused in British minds; Englishmen now sought to find their ancestors and their conquerors, the Romans. Catalogues and descriptions were made of surviving monuments and wild guesses made about the builders. The antiquaries have endowed us with many a false impression about the past, as well as some of the finest works of art which were brought back from their journeys abroad.

Thus were the first attempts to find Roman Britain. The remains do not rival those in other parts of the Roman world in magnificence. Many have been looted for building stone by subsequent generations. Some Roman settlements have been built over and obliterated in the rubble of foundations. What is surprising is not that the remains are sparse, but that any survive at all.

If the remains lack the spectacle of those in Africa, Rome or Greece, they encourage the spirit of adventure, as a foundation here or a fragment of mosaic there is discovered in a pub yard or the wall of a boutique. Lurking under allotment gardens or suburban villas lie wild, improbable scenes of pagan gods and sea creatures, petrified in the tesserae of mosaics. In the cellars of High Street shops surrounded by boxes of merchandise and the incongruous muddle of staff coffee-breaks lie the columns of huge public halls against which usurpers like Magnus Maximus would have leant while inciting the people to rebellion. In quiet cornfields masses of grey stone and rubble rise up twenty feet above the hedges, the masonry only slightly weathered, the mortar still intact. For the adventurous, walking in some of the more remote and bleak countryside, a few stones and hollows in the heather point unerringly to the presence of men from Dacia, Gaul, Egypt or Africa who came, saw and changed for ever the edge of the civilised world.

1 The Roads to Rome

The majority of Roman roads are now obliterated by modern highways or vegetation. They varied from simple tracks to the substantial foundations of larger stones or slabs covered with rammed gravel. A superb stretch of moorland road will delight the energetic walker on Blackstone Edge in Lancashire. Enjoyment of this site will probably depend, except for the keenest of antiquarian spirits, on the weather. In the right conditions the road can be observed as a light green strip on the hillside. Near the summit, fine sturdy cobblestones with a prominent and deliberately dressed central groove emerge from the grass. This unusually constructed road has survived destruction by animals, climate and vandals. Graffiti on the stones go back to 1882 at least. (One section of road desecrated in 1965 bears to their eternal shame the names of P. MacHugh and I. Hartig.) It will be no surprise to anyone who visits the site that the Romans found the path too steep, and at some stage abandoned it for a more sensible zigzag route nearby. Along this more orthodox path came the waggons and horsemen, footsoldiers and traders. After a journey through the Pennines, some of the bleakest countryside in Britain, many a heart must have quickened or pack seemed lighter as the fort of Mamucium (Manchester) was sighted. The threat of ambush would not have been idle in this area, where the Brigantes tribe constantly resisted the force of civilisation.

It is traditionally thought that Roman roads were straight.

Indeed, many that have survived in any readily visible form are remarkable for their adherence to the lines between surveyors' points. A large number of unusually straight roads (excluding motorways) will be found to follow the lines of Roman originals. Nevertheless, not all straight roads are Roman and not all Roman roads are straight. The remarkable series of aerial photographs of the Fens shows a network of winding tracks in common use in the Roman period, belying G. K. Chesterton's assertion that it was

Before the Roman came to Rye, or out to Severn strode,
The rolling English drunkard made the rolling English road.

The name Ermine Street, along with the names of other such famous Roman highways as Fosse Way, Watling Street and Akeman Street, was not that used by the Romans but by the Saxons. By the tenth century many parish boundaries were delineated by old Roman roads. Many a suspiciously straight boundary or hedgerow will prove on inspection of nothing more obscure than an Ordnance Survey map to be of Roman origin. Some highways were kept open after the Roman period—names such as Streat, Port Way or Sarn Helen (the last in Wales) usually refer to Roman routes. Confusingly the famous Ermine Street has a sister Ermin Street from Speen to Cirencester, Watling Street (Kent to Wroxeter in Salop) is duplicated from Wroxeter to Kenchester, and Akeman Street is found from Tring to Cirencester, from Cambridge to Ely, and along Fleet Street and the Strand.

A journey through the flat Lincolnshire countryside along the A1 from Stamford as far north as Colsterworth follows the line of a Roman road now known as Ermine Street. Just north of this village the Roman road is followed by the B6403. Passing directly through the village (and Roman town) of Ancaster, it eventually continues as a ride through the fields. For a distance the B road is raised about four feet above the ploughed fields, which are broken by small woods. Here pheasants strut and call, themselves probably the descendants of birds introduced to Britain by the Romans. The road height is gained by the Roman *agger* or bank which improved the drainage.

Milestones were placed at intervals along Roman roads, for the aid of travellers and the glorification of those repairing or building the highways. Some four to six feet high, these columns were generally inscribed with the titles and names of the emperor and the numeral of mileage. They frequently omit the place from which the miles were measured.

Six milestones have been found from one of the most dramatic periods in British history, AD 287–293. The Channel coasts appear to have been infested with pirates and a Menapian called Carausius was appointed to remove the threat. Apparently he failed in his task, for his arrest was ordered. Medieval sources relate that he abused his office and allowed the pirates to make raids, subsequently seizing their booty for himself. Whatever the truth, he defied the Emperor by winning over the British and establishing a breakaway state. For six years he ruled, apparently with much success, for roads were repaired and the coinage reformed. A milestone, found in 1894 near Carlisle, reads IMP C M AVR MAVS CARAVSIO P F INVICTO AVG (The imperial Caesar, Marcus Aurelius Mausaenus Carausius, Dutiful and Fortunate, the undefeated Augustus). The confidence displayed on this stone was shortlived, typically of the period, his reign was brought to an end when his colleague Allectus murdered him. After the province had finally been brought into the Empire once again, in 296, the milestone was inverted and reinscribed.

INNS

Posting Stations—small inns which closely resembled Youth Hostels, in that the traveller was expected to provide equipment such as bedding—were situated along the course of roads. At a period when it was common to travel in one day distances that motorists are now restricted to covering in an hour, these *mansiones* were vital. Less spartan accommodation was to be found in town inns.

One fine example of an inn can be seen outside the fort at Vindolanda (Chesterholm, Northumberland). I arrived there by car at Easter-time 1975. By the time I had waded across the muddy track to the temporary hut that housed souvenirs, guide-books and ticket office, I was at least as cold and miserable as any Roman arriving on foot or horseback. The northern winds appeared to be attempting to complete the task of flattening the walls, already so well accomplished by Time. In the mire and the rain, the walls consolidated to two feet at the most, the mansio resembled a holidaymaker's nightmare vision of a half-built hotel. All traces of the comfort afforded by the fifteen rooms grouped round a courtyard had disappeared. The small heated dining-room, the kitchen with its stone oven from which had come so many hot meals, the gaily painted wall-plaster of red and blue geometric designs in one of the bedrooms, was now reduced to notes in an archaeologist's file. Where now was the cameraderie of a latrine to seat eight people, astonishing to modern minds inhibited by an ideal of privacy? Fortunately even on such an unattractive day the other features of this fort made it worthy of a visit (see p 123).

2 Carpets in Stone

The most consistently beautiful and impressive of all Roman remains in Britain are the mosaic floors. Pieces of stone, tile, pottery or even glass were set into mortar on a rubble bed to form lasting pictures of mythological scenes, gods and goddesses, or simply attractive patterns. The remains of over 750 of these status symbols have come to light—some painstakingly removed to museums, others restored in situ, and sadly, many vandalised and lost.

The accounts of early antiquaries constantly refer to mosaics destroyed by the plough or torn apart by the populace. William Stukeley the antiquary records a mosaic discovered on 25 January 1712 near Akeman Street as

> A most curious tesselated pavement for bulk and beauty the most considerable we know of; it was a parallelogram 35 foot long and 20 foot wide, a noble room, and no doubt designed for feasting and jolity—in one of the circular works was Bacchus represented in stones properly coloured, with a tiger, a thyrsus in his hand enwrapped with vine leaves.

Tragically the landlord and tenant disagreed over sharing the profits of showing it to the public and the latter 'maliciously tore it to pieces'. Although from the eighteenth century onwards many dilettantes and antiquaries were intent on preserving ancient objects, not so the 'ignorant vulgar' of Stukeley's narrative. Some at least were sufficiently avaricious to charge fees for viewing, a flaw in character that has presumably accounted for some mosaics being preserved to the present day.

It is through the procession of nereids and nymphs, cupids and goddesses, peltas and swastikas that we can follow the gradual seduction of the Britons by Rome. Mosaic floors epitomise all things Roman. Where they occur, the least that can be said is that the owner was pro-Roman in outlook. Before the conquest some of the southern British tribes had imported wine and artworks, pottery and jewels, but none had ever become rich or romanised enough to own a mosaic pavement.

After that fateful year AD 43, the rewards of allegiance to the invaders can be traced within forty years by a short but splendid proliferation of mosaics, mostly put down by highly skilled foreign craftsmen. A lull in the industry followed, presumably as the province of Britannia struggled to its economic feet. People who had hitherto depended on raiding and rustling had to learn to live in the newly established towns, to earn civilised livings, and to adhere to Roman laws. With strong Roman encouragement towns grew up in the Lowlands, well protected by the military zone of Wales and northern Britain. By AD 150 or thereabouts, mosaicists were again in demand to adorn the town houses of officials or romanised chieftains. Between AD 200 and 300 the industry once more went into recession—presumably in some way connected with the general political instability of the period, but a tremendous boom followed in the fourth century. British craftsmen whose ancestors would have been putting their artistic talents into producing battle helmets, torcs or shields were now pitting their wits against the classical art of mosaic laying. Schools centred on or near Cirencester, Dorchester, Brough-on-Humber and Water Newton reached their peaks in succession throughout the century, and evolved distinctive provincial styles.

Mosaics were not the floors to which every Romano-Briton might aspire. Flooring ranged from simple beaten earth or flagging to *opus sectile* (coarse tesserae of one colour only), or the finest *opus vermiculatum* (with tesserae only a quarter of an inch in diameter). Mosaics were the result of great financial outlay and deliberation over design. Although patterns were stereotyped through being copied from pattern books it was unusual in Britain to buy ready-made sections (*emblemata*). One mosaic from Verulamium (St Albans) was obviously manufactured elsewhere and put down in sections since the pattern is not regular, but most seem to have been laid down where and as required. Mosaicists tended to establish a set repertoire to be varied according to fashion or need.

The colours available were dictated largely by native geology. Purbeck marble (also used for building purposes) gave dark blues, reds and greens; limestones could range from grey to brown; lower greensand gave a pleasant green. Where black was required, often for emphasising features or outlining figures, Kimmeridge shale could be employed, and white was achieved by using hard chalk. Some mosaics have the rather strong, sombre hues of Victorian solemnity; dark red with grey or black emphasised in creams.

In the Corinium Museum in Cirencester a reconstructed workshop allows the visitor to see a lifesize model of a stonemason at work chipping suitable tesserae from sticks of prepared stone.

FIRST-CENTURY MOSAICS

Among the early patrons of mosaicists one man in particular was ahead not only of his British peers but also of most of the Empire. Between AD 75 and 80, mosaics were ordered for his palatial villa at Fishbourne, Sussex. They were crisply and strikingly black and white, with the interest lying in the diaper and lozenge patterns and the square or cruciform motifs. The fussy, colourful floors that had been developed from Greek originals five centuries previously were out of fashion in the Empire.

18

About the same time a further extravagance led to four more colourful mosaics being ordered and laid at Fishbourne. One of these was manufactured in *opus vermiculatum*, a technique which required craftsmen of the highest skill, who could handle the many subtle colours required and could vary the shapes of the tesserae to give depth to the picture. The result was a charming confection of rosettes and vine leaves in a circle, with an outer border of two-strand guilloche. The pinks and subtle greens on a light background give the mosaic an appearance not unlike a petrified Chinese carpet. The corners of the dark bordering squares that surround the roundel enclose wine cups (*canthari*), dolphins and tendrils, but sadly the central part of the floor was worn through in Roman times. It is so far unique in design, and the two-strand guilloche was ahead of its time by several decades.

These mosaics were made possible because of the peculiar history of the tribe of the Atrebates whose leader apparently lived at Fishbourne. Almost certainly the name of this highly romanised man was Cogidubnus—his name and Roman title REX appear on an inscription from Chichester. The Atrebates had long enjoyed good relationships with Rome before the Claudian conquest. One of their kings, Verica, (c AD 10–40) had even inscribed his coin with a vine leaf (a later reflection of which can perhaps be seen in the mosaic described above). The use of this motif was presumably to indicate the flourishing wine trade with Rome.

The Romans had first come into contact with the continental branch of the Atrebates during the Gallic campaigns of Julius Caesar, and had set up a certain Commius as tribal leader. In 55 and 54 BC this man was sent as envoy to Britain by Caesar, but tantalisingly much is left out of the story in the terse military reports. We learn of misunderstandings and a false arrest, and the final climax when the British leader, Cassivellaunus, was cornered by the Romans at Wheathampstead near St Albans. Surrender was inevitable, but only Commius was of sufficient diplomatic stature to mediate.

After such service to Rome, Commius inexplicably changed his allegiances and fought in the Gallic rebellion. The Romans retaliated with two attempts on his life and finally he surrendered on condition that he never had to look another Roman in the face. This melodramatic decision was apparently never revoked. Within a short while Caesar was pursuing him towards waiting ships on the north French coast. Freedom was almost in sight but the tide was out and the ships were grounded. Rising to the occasion with all the dash to be expected of a great barbarian leader, Commius ordered the sails to be hoisted. The Romans, thinking him to be afloat, abandoned the chase and Commius sailed away on the next tide to found a dynasty of Atrebatic kings in Britain.

The sons of his old age, Tincommius, Eppillus and Verica, pursued increasingly friendly policies with Rome: Verica and Tincommius even fled from their own tribe to the Empire. It is possibly not too far-fetched to suggest that the young Cogidubnus himself, if not one of his forebears, was taken as hostage in AD 43 —perhaps he fled with Verica in that year—and was brought up in the Empire, possibly in Rome itself. This attractive fable might account for the highly developed classical taste displayed in the Fishbourne mosaics of the first century.

Fig 1   Mosaic from Fishbourne, Sussex

Such were the fortunes of those who aided the Romans. For the rebels and dissenters, people like the Brigantes or the Iceni, four centuries of unrest were in store. Standards of living were eroded as deprivations and retaliations disrupted the traditional ways of life. Their stories are not to be discovered in mosaics but we will encounter some of them later.

THE URBAN BOOM, AD 100–200

Of the second-century mosaics, none surpass those from the fine town of Verulamium (St Albans). Some time between AD 160 and 190 one householder ordered eight square feet of lovely

Fig 2   Oceanus from a mosaic at St Albans

mosaic flooring. Quiet shades of red, white, grey, buff and black were used with great delicacy for an almost perfectly drawn geometric border with four rosettes in the corners and four chalices in panels. The centre displays the strongly drawn head of a sea-god, Oceanus, with powerful brown and grey neck muscles. Unfortunately, lack of intermediary shades led to a certain coarseness in their execution. The god's hair flows freely and merges with a white beard, stark against his rugged brown face. To cater for more abstract tastes a colourful drawing of a shell took someone's fancy between AD 130 and 150, and mine in 1974. An orange background sets off the white, blue and mauve flutes, the white, yellow and orange ears and white hinge.

Fig 3   Fountain from a mosaic at St Albans

A much more jolly scene in mosaic from the same town is that known as the Fountain. Two dolphins leap from a yellow chalice which spurts pale blue water in two jets. Their tails have become entangled with the chalice handles and their snouts, fins and tail prongs highlight the entire scene in scarlet.

THE FOURTH CENTURY AND MOSAIC SCHOOLS

After about AD 300 Romano-Britons let the fashion of mosaic floor laying go to their heads. The natives, probably aided by continental-trained craftsmen, specialised both in technique and subject matter. The variety of subjects available to customers was overwhelming.

Customers with fairly primitive taste were catered for by the Petuarian (Brough-on-Humber) school. Only a handful of mosaics from this area are known—a common feature is the wheel design, an echo of the St Andrew's Cross found in the greatest of the British schools, Corinium. This prolific workshop, which, like the others has not been discovered except by inference from the artistic designs employed in the area surrounding the town, abounded in portrayals of Orpheus with attendant animals and birds.

The Durnovarian school is unmistakable from the numerous portrayals of marine creatures—of which dolphins are prominent.

Archaeology has little in common with astronomy except in-so-far as the Woodchester mosaic is concerned. To see this superb 49ft square in which 'Another Orpheus sings again', mosaic addicts must wait at least twelve years between 'sitings'. The mosaic was last exposed in its findspot under Woodchester churchyard in Gloucestershire in 1973. The pattern is sophisticated and exceptionally complicated as befitted the palatial villa of which it adorned the chief reception room. Four columns held up the roof—the base of one is still intact within the mosaic. Only Orpheus' left leg remains, the lyre resting on his knee. The inner frieze of his roundel has a procession of birds —a pheasant, peacock, dove and duck. The outer frieze displays a bear, winged griffin and horse. In the space between the roundel and the wide outer border of the square, near the column, are two water nymphs in diaphanous clothes leaning on an urn.

The traditional art of the Celtic craftsman sometimes creeps into the classical pictures of the time. Celtic (British) art was essentially abstract whether in sculpture or metalwork. The British artist was as disinterested in naturalism as Salvador Dali, or Picasso in his Cubist period. What is sometimes mistaken for bad drawing was often simply the native artist's avowal of the supreme unimportance of the exact shape of things. The resultant mosaics although ugly and comical if viewed in classical terms are livelier and in many ways more attractive if dispassionately assessed. Thus the sterile beauty of the Venus from Bignor, Sussex, has little of the good humour or gaiety of the same goddess from Rudston, now in Hull museum. The head of the Bignor Venus, albeit heavily restored, stares at the viewer with classical coldness. The bust is untraditionally and modestly swathed up to the chin. The Rudston lady, lacking only the shell symbolic of the goddess' birth from the waves, is dressed in nothing but her bangles. Her hair flows freely and youthfully, but her figure is already beginning to spread at the hips. Her mirror has been discarded. Her expression of extreme concentration is suggestive less of a confident goddess of love, than of a Romano-British woman determined to relive her youth. In this mosaic her wish is perpetuated as permanently as possible.

One of my favourite mosaics in Britain is a good-natured piece in Leeds City Museum, whence it was brought from the town of Aldborough. The subject is the mythical she-wolf who suckled Romulus and Remus. This particular mosaic looks as though it were drawn by a child, and indeed it is nice to think

Fig 4 She-wolf from a mosaic at Rudston, Yorks

that perhaps some fond romanised member of the Brigantes tribe had the doodle of a favourite offspring translated for posterity into grey, red and yellow stones. The wolf certainly bears little resemblance to any living animal, with its cat-like ears and the elegant flanks of a racehorse. She crosses her paws nonchalantly, and smiles broadly at the observer.

Gentle, good-natured scenes are a feature of British mosaics. The pictures of races or the amphitheatre that can be so gruesome in other parts of the Empire as to defy one to imagine people actually eating while looking at them, are totally absent. The few examples that do exist are generally innocuous.

Gladiators depicted in a mosaic still to be seen at Bignor, Sussex, are lively cupids. The most dramatic picture of games, now in the British Museum, was found at Horkstow, Lincolnshire. A splendid chariot race is in progress; beautiful drawn horses in buff, red and bluish-grey prance and toss their heads. A wheel has fallen off one of the chariots and the driver spills out to be helped by another as his steed gallops on. The scene takes place in a typical Roman racecourse. The track hugs a central *spina* or line of columns with dangerously sharp hairpin bends at each end. The Horkstow charioteers are less well drawn, suggesting that the artist's greater interest was in the animals. The scene might reflect the local horse-rearing industry, or have a more mystical meaning. The addition of the god Orpheus indicates that this might represent the race of life with the final victory of the soul at the end.

The Horkstow mosaic is one of many to have double meanings. When Constantine the Great declared Christianity to be the official Roman religion in AD 313, mosaicists saw no reason to change their repertoire, and patrons continued to commission well-loved pagan or mythological motifs. Figures of Orpheus could now be used as the Good Shepherd, Bacchus and his cantharus were almost identical to Christ with a chalice. Several examples have been found where Christian symbols are juxtaposed with pagan. A famous mosaic, now not visible, from Frampton, Dorset, contains a large Chi-Rho (the first two letters of the Greek word for Christ), and an inscription in praise of Cupid.

THE MEN BEHIND THE MOSAICS

Only occasionally do the owners of mosaics assert their personalities. One mosaicist (probably called Terentius), felt it necessary to put his monogram on an example of his art at Bignor TᴙR. At Low Ham an exceptional mosaic (now in the Castle Museum at Taunton) was discovered in 1946. Although not so finely executed as that at Woodchester it shows scenes taken from Virgil's *Aeneid*. The mosaic is arranged in a series of four panels around the figure of Venus. The complex story of human and immortal passions apparently overwhelmed the artist, for the details are not well drawn and the expressions on the faces positively invite the viewer to add new captions. Venus' eyebrow has been forgotten as though she applied her make-up in haste. Nonetheless, the mosaic suggests a patron of highly developed classical tastes. Perhaps he was a man in the same mould as T Avidius Quietus, governor of Britain from about AD 97–100, who is known to have been acquainted with Plutarch. The ideal of classical study which perhaps led to the copying of a manuscript model at Low Ham has been somewhat marred by the circumstances of the discovery. The lovers, Dido and Aeneas, were disturbed by a farmer digging a grave for a diseased sheep.

THE LAST MOSAICS

Mosaics were laid down in Britain until the very last years of the fourth century and possibly even later. A worn coin of Theodosius was found in the mortar of a geometric mosaic at Hucclecote, proving it to have been laid down sometime around AD 385, only twenty-five years before the final dissociation of the Romans with the province of Britannia. This was precisely the period when Magnus Maximus was inciting the British troops to cross the Channel and make a bid for freedom. Despite the incursions of barbarians across the frontiers at this time, the Romano-Britons felt secure enough to lay down fine floors in their villas. They deliberated over the choice of a flamboyant style or a more restrained drawing while the Picts overran the northern frontier, the Saxons were repelled from strongholds along the east coast, and Roman fought Roman on the Continent. Values in the Roman period can sometimes be hard to understand.

3 A Place in the Country

The first villa for which I searched proved to be as much an anti-climax as the first fort of Lympne. I chose it at random, partly through having family connections with the area and partly through having found in the recesses of an attic a greying guidebook with rusty staples published in 1938. The villa was at Rudston in Yorkshire, and there was nothing at all to be seen at the site. In this respect at least, Rudston is typical of the majority. Villas are often a disappointment structurally to those who expect the remains of halcyon days spent idly picking fat grapes and lingering in beflowered courtyards watching fountains play. This sort of idyll was no doubt lived out by a few privileged people in Britain, but as in most large country establishments the principal pastime in a villa was work. Villas were viable economic units, and the term covers a wide variety of buildings from modest barn-like structures and cottages to vast palaces. They are best described by the umbrella term 'a place in the country'. House extensions were common and sprawling edifices that would have made a modern architect shudder, evolved over centuries as time and money permitted.

Naturally no one type of person lived in villas. Bailiffs or managers ran some for town-based owners, others were worked by British farmers. They tend to be closely connected with the towns, presumably both for the owner's convenience and for ease of distributing produce. Villa owners owed much of their prosperity to nearby commercial enterprises. The fine villas of

Fig 5   Reconstruction of a typical Roman villa

the Nene valley must have been financed by the potteries. Others were connected with mining, forestry or agriculture alone. The richer owners enjoyed wine, fine imported table-wares and works of art, but villas also housed the shepherds and the cattle ranchers, ploughmen, lumberjacks and labourers. Some appear to have been worked by slaves and many were required to supply the troops. Taxes in the form of cattle or corn may account for the apparent poverty of some villas in good agricultural areas. Salisbury Plain, Cranbourne Chase, and the vast area drained and developed by the Romans in the Fens were strangely devoid of villas. Perhaps these were the imperial estates known to have existed in the province.

Villas built on Roman lines from the start are a feature of the romanised south. None have been found north of Durham and the handful from Wales are in the south.

IN THE DINING-ROOM

One of the best ways of determining the extent of romanisation is by the prevalence of the dining-room. Roman manners demanded that dining was the pinnacle of the civilised man's day, and the finest mosaics are usually found in this room, the *triclinium*. The importance of feasting is demonstrated in almost every museum in the country by the very fine tableware of pottery, pewter or even solid silver.

Whereas the Celts apparently ate outside sitting on the ground, and many Britons would have continued to sit down to meals, a true Roman reclined on couches placed around the walls of the typical dining-room. Normally nine people were arranged thus in order of importance. The walls of British villas and town-houses were often painted in abstract panels to represent natural stones (cheaper than the real thing), or in plain expanses of colour, or with gentle rural scenes.

When the Romans first considered invading Britain, they were naturally interested in the 'rewards of victory', as Tacitus called exports. Once the conquest was established, many goods were imported too and enjoyed, not the least of which was pottery.

In the first two centuries the finest pottery came from Gaul— the justly famous samian ware, with its distinctive red gloss. The sheen on this luxury ware is unique, the result of minute fragments of mica in the clays. Futile attempts were made in London and Colchester, and in this century at Bath, to imitate the ware. Possibly the most famous and spectacular collection is to be seen at Rowley's House Museum in Shrewsbury. Here can be seen the nests of samian vessels found in the excavation of the Forum at Wroxeter, just as they were stacked up ready for sale.

On the night of 31 December AD 192 the emperor Commodus was assassinated, and feasting in the Empire was never the same again. The political chaos that ensued affected every rich man's table in Britain, and many a Romano-Briton must have regretted that he had ever developed his classical taste, now that the requisite wines and pottery were no longer available. Britain was closely involved in the politics, for in AD 193 the governor of the province, Clodius Albinus (highly supported in senatorial quarters) dared to claim the purple, with the backing of the three legions in Britain and one in Spain. His opponents were Pescennius Niger in Syria who held nine legions and L Septimius Severus in Pannonia who held the allegiance of sixteen legions. Albinus' bid bordered on the reckless. Severus sensibly gave him the title of Caesar (implying his right of succession) and marched to defeat Niger in 194. Incredibly, Albinus seems to have believed him and, escaping the assassination attempt that was bound to follow, proclaimed himself Augustus. He crossed the Channel and was eventually defeated in a hard-fought battle. Albinus was killed and Severus punished his followers with confiscations. The wine trade between Britain and Spain was decimated. The pottery industry on the continent, overrun and disrupted by the general disorder as well as falling standards, went into rapid decay. Britons had to find alternative ways of enjoying their feasts.

From this period onwards, wines from the Moselle and Bordeaux were common and beer was drunk in huge tankards holding a quart or more. Pewter began to find favour; the Cornish tin industry was revived and other pottery was imported from abroad. Rich and beautifully lustred Rhenish wares came into fashion after about AD 175, and the British pottery industries flourished.

Hounds pursue game in perpetuity on some Castor ware, iced onto the surface of the pot as on a cake. Face urns have smiling faces that peep out of many museum cases. The names and careers of some potters are known from the makers' stamps on their products. C Attius Marinus, for example, began work at Colchester, moved briefly to the vicinity of St Albans and having built up a flourishing business there, finally settled at Hartshill in Warwickshire.

Intricately and minutely designed glassware was frequently imported from Syria or Alexandria. Most glass in Britain was for window panes—furnaces have been found in many places. Other glass vessels held unguents or perfumes.

At some time in the fourth century some educated person in Somerset owned a really fine glass bowl with an inscription in a mixture of Greek and Latin round the rim. It reads 'Long Life to you and yours, drink and good health to you'. The bottom of the bowl has a freehand engraving of a hunt scene. A horseman gallops between the trees followed by two short-haired hounds closely pursuing a hare. His short tunic is decorated with small circles and his cloak flies behind him in the wind. Texture has been given to the figures by pin-point scratches and even the shadows have been minutely observed.

Even the food itself was decorated. In the collection of the Duke of Wellington on loan to Reading Museum is a small cake mould from Silchester, capital of the Atrebates. Once baked the cake would have displayed a fairly intricate design of imperial personages. From the hairstyles the design probably represents Septimius Severus and his wife Julia Domna, who are making

Fig 6 Maenad on the great silver dish from the Mildenhall Treasure. Fourth century AD

a sacrifice to the gods. This could well have been used for cakes made for a thanksgiving service for the emperor's victory in Britain. The Atrebates were not being backward in establishing their gratitude to the emperor and orthodox authority.

Treasures like the silverware found at Mildenhall, Suffolk, adorned the tables of the very rich. Now in the British Museum the thirty-four silver objects are of exceptional splendour. The most famous item is a dish, nearly 2ft in diameter, which must have caused many a steward to stagger under its weight of $18\frac{1}{4}$lb. The god Oceanus stares out of the centre, accompanied by four dolphins hiding in his hair, and figures of nereids, sea centaurs and beasts surround him. Bacchus stands with his foot on a panther, Silenus carries a wine cup, Hercules is completely drunk. The scene of extraordinary disorder is brought into classical control by the artistry of the silversmith.

HEATING SYSTEMS

Hypocausts are the central heating systems for which the Romans are deservedly famous. By raising the floor on tile or stone stilts, hot air from furnaces stoked by coal, peat or wood could be circulated throughout the rooms. It was a simple system, although no doubt highly wasteful in terms of fuel economy. Stukeley observing the system from the eighteenth century announced 'This is an excellent invention for heating a room and might well be introduced amongst us in winter time.' In fact, only twentieth-century technology has been able to improve on the method. Hypocausts have often been well preserved, despite the attentions of such notables as the eighteenth-century Lord Coningsby who adorned the floor of his evidence room with their tiles.

Bathing was a communal and therapeutic pastime, and water was much in demand on all Roman sites. In the various baths available friends could be met and conversed with, and the aches

Plate 1 (left) Hadrian's Wall near Housesteads Fort, Northumberland. *(Janet Bord)*

Plate 2 (right) Latrines at Housesteads (Vercovicium). *(Janet Bord)*

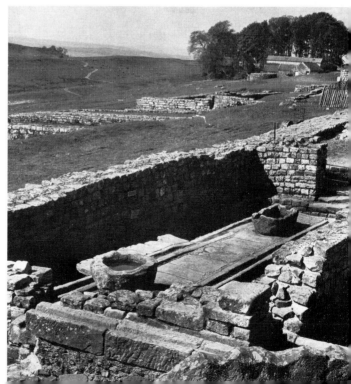

Plate 3 (left) A stone head from Towcester, Northamptonshire. This portrays an underworld goddess and has a strong Celtic influence. *(British Museum)*

Plate 4 (right) A classical head, possibly of Germanicus, found in Bosham harbour, Sussex. Dated first century AD, it is made of marble. *(British Museum)*

of the day removed. All forts and towns had elaborate bathing establishments, actively encouraged by the authorities who were well aware that cleanliness and relaxation are important necessities where large numbers of people live together. The bath suite often consisted of an undressing room, a warm room, a hot room, a cold room and a cold plunge, which altogether would have ensured that the members of the household were clean. The method of bathing was to sweat out all the excess dirt, cover the body with oils, and scrape both dirt and oil off with toilet instruments. Hot baths as they are conceived of today were not in the order of things. Wright, the nineteenth-century excavator of the town of Wroxeter, in explaining to his readers about Roman bathing habits, decided that 'in fact the bather was treated somewhat in the same way as we now treat horses when they come into the stable hot'. Strigils (fearsome-looking implements) and other toilet articles are frequent finds on Roman sites. Many look to eyes used to nothing more stringent than foam sponges and flannels as though they would have been better used in the stable even in Roman times; others are more delicate. On a holiday quest for King Arthur at Glastonbury I idly glanced at a museum case full of Saxon wall plaster. In one corner were two very delicate implements of iron, thinner than matches, with tiny detailed terminals—Roman ear cleaners, indispensable to someone spending an afternoon at the public baths.

INNOVATIONS

Roman ways permeated even further than the dining-room. Some traditional establishments were updated gradually, occasionally so subtly that it is difficult to recognise the change. Even the methods of farming were improved. Ploughs were more efficient than ever before and the Romano-British farmer was introduced to such modern conveniences as iron-tipped spades, rakes and scythes. Corn-drying furnaces became a popular method of beating bad harvests. The Romans introduced new plants: rye, oats, vetch, flax, cabbage, parsnip, turnip, carrots, celery, and possibly others. Gardens, not a feature of traditional British houses, now grew violets, poppies, pansies, roses and lilies. In the kitchen gardens bees hummed and apple trees, vines, mulberries and walnuts gave untraditional shade.

It is probably best to visit villas as though visiting a building site on which the foundations have recently been laid. Sizes are deceptive without walls, and the protective sheds covering many detract from the unity. When standing, villas resembled medieval half-timbered buildings in many ways. Courtyards were popular, many buildings being extended to produce such an enclosure. The exteriors were covered with stucco or plaster, though some were entirely made of stone.

A NATIVE HOMESTEAD

At Din Lligwy in Anglesey the walls of a typical, slightly romanised settlement stand to about 6ft in places, sheltered by trees. It is an enchanting site, well grassed with naturally crumbling stonework. The consolidation has merged well with the surroundings. The sole concession to Roman taste is in the shape of the huts. Whereas British Celtic tradition would have demanded round houses, some chieftain in the fourth century gave this farmstead a modern look by enclosing the traditionally circular huts and four rectangular ones in a pentagonal wall. The result was as far removed from a Roman villa as 'Georgian town houses' of the 1970s are from eighteenth-century mansions.

A PALATIAL VILLA

A palatial Roman home was found in 1961 at Fishbourne in Sussex. The site was already threatened by road works and known to be Roman, but the extent and luxury of the accommodation had not been guessed. The villa started life as a military base, well within the area of safety afforded by the pro-Roman Atrebates. Within a few years the supply depot had been replaced by a house which boasted wall plaster in the Roman style. In the '60s a further masonry house was erected with mosaic floors.

The house or palace in which Cogidubnus possibly lived and in which the splendid mosaics already described (p 18) were laid down was the product of building work after AD 75. Fishbourne's structural history was thus typical of many houses, though exaggeratedly rapid. In the final palace, ten acres of rooms and gardens were designed to accommodate the 'prince' and his many retainers, his family, official visitors and craftsmen.

I arrived at the site in 1975 on a day when the place was miraculously deserted except for the ticket collectors and café staff. I walked across the vast gravelled approach to the entrance hall that is impressively well kept and superbly fitted out. Rooms led off it on three sides, with lights and beautiful objects visible through their glass doors. A model of the palace stood on a table to the right, and guidebooks were on sale. This was merely the modern ticket office.

The villa itself, I reasoned, must indeed be an experience in hedonism, a sort of ideal home exhibition covering the period c AD 75 to AD 280 when the place was burnt down. Alas, even this villa is structurally unimpressive. Somehow the huge barn-like covering erected so apparently effortlessly in the twentieth century makes a mockery of the fifteen or so rooms that were once the north wing of the palace. As a casual visitor I found the relaid mosaics and consolidated walls difficult to decipher.

As a feast of beautiful Roman objects however the villa is unparalleled in Britain. Set in an easily accessible situation, it has all the facilities that anyone could hope for on a day's relaxation, come rain or shine. In the dimly-lit museum pottery,

37

metalwork, glass and photographs of the excavation glow like jewels in their bright cases. From the overpowering capital, so huge I failed to see it the first time round, to the details so common in all Roman museums of hob-nailed boot prints on tiles, all is set out. There are slides and commentaries, reconstructions, and a picture of the excavator asleep in a wheelbarrow.

The exposed wing of the villa itself in its shed is crossed by catwalks. Mosaic after mosaic from the most fragmentary to the almost complete are revealed. Fishbourne beats the record for the most mosaics in one house, long held by the twenty previously found at North Leigh, Oxfordshire. The glass shelter leads through into gardens stocked with Roman herbs and plants that have now become established. The half of the garden that is free from modern buildings makes a pleasant park in summer.

In the time of Cogidubnus guests would have walked through an impressive entrance hall, past an ornamental pond and into an open courtyard, 300ft wide. To left and right lawns and flowers would have led the eye beyond the wings on either side with their rows of columns to the centre of the west wing. Here raised above the garden was the audience chamber in which homage could be paid, diplomatic messages could be heard and guests could be received.

As might be expected in such a large establishment, there was a change of owners around AD 100. If this is indeed the home of Cogidubnus, then the previous establishments on the site can be regarded as manifestations of his rise in prosperity.

The destruction came some time between 270 and 290, the very period when Carausius the Menapian (p 14) was ruling a British Empire. Could it be that Fishbourne was destroyed during this period of unrest? Had the Atrebates so long the champions of Rome finally backed the losing side? Whatever the truth the end of the house of Commius appears to have come and Fishbourne was a ruin ripe for plunder. The wall plaster peeled and decayed, flint was ripped out down to the wall footings, and by AD 320 the palace that had once entertained officials from all over the Empire and had employed some of the greatest craftsmen known to the western world, was nothing but a grassy ruin.

A COURTYARD VILLA

A less extraordinary villa, but arguably the best preserved in Britain, lies in a singularly cold position at Chedworth, near the

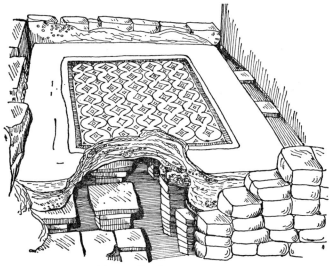

Fig 7 Chedworth mosaic

Roman town of Cirencester. We owe the preservation of this site to a gamekeeper searching for a lost ferret in the woods of Lord Eldon's estate in 1864. Pieces of pavement were revealed, and excavations took place. Part of the exposed areas were covered and roofed with very substantial brick sheds and eventually, in 1924, the entire site and the museum that had been built within it were given to the National Trust.

Further excavations followed, and the exact history of the

villa was reappraised. Sadly, one of the most beautiful finds of all the early excavations is now lost. This famous swan-necked spoon in silver was inscribed with the words CENSORINE GAVDEAS (Censorinus Rejoice!). It has been suggested that one of the owners of the villa might have been the Censorinus thus fêted.

Typically, Chedworth began life in the early second century when the troops still required a supply of corn and cattle as they pressed into the north. There followed three phases of alteration, the first after a fire, until in the late fourth century the villa had both an inner garden and an outer courtyard, a very extensive suite of baths and a new dining-room.

The dining-room, as it is now exposed to the public, is as it would have appeared (except for the presence of walls, furniture and people) in the early fourth century. A lovely Cirencester School mosaic adorns its floor with three boyish figures representing Spring, Summer and Winter dancing in triangular frames. A drain runs away from one corner of the dining-room—a labour-saving device for ancient housekeeping. A shrine in one corner started life dedicated to water nymphs and was converted to Christianity.

A VILLA WITH A VIOLENT HISTORY

Lullingstone (p 100) is a very attractive corner of Roman Britain. Like Fishbourne, the villa has the advantages of being covered over and served by a car park. The ruins have considerable character, chiefly due to the extent of one cellar room known accurately if unpoetically as the Deep Room. When the Romans arrived the valley of the Derwent was cultivated by a British farmer. Within forty years a new house, with flint and mortar walls, replaced what must have been a simple home of wattle and daub. The Deep Room was probably a grain store.

This simple romanised dwelling stood in an elevated position above the river on a low terrace cut into the slope. It was to its position that the villa owes its preservation—over the years clay and soil crept down covering the walls in some cases still 8ft high.

By the end of the century the owner was fully romanised, but his classical tastes were overshadowed by his successor. In about AD 180 the house fell into the hands of a rich and sophisticated owner of Mediterranean origin. We have a rare glimpse of the kind of family who lived in the villa from two portraits that have survived a chequered career and are now in the British Museum. The best preserved depicts a patrician of about forty-five years old, wearing semi-military dress. Since it was almost certainly made before AD 135, it must have been an heirloom.

Such a family needed more than a mere provincial farmhouse and accordingly the villa was fitted out with a suite of baths, kitchens and cult rooms (p 101). The Deep Room became a shrine to the water nymphs, and the thatched roof was transformed with red tiles relieved with a few of decorative yellow. The estate would have provided this half-timbered bungalow with fish, timber, corn and cattle, and the family enjoyed a high standard of living. Meal-times were brightened by samian pottery and Castor ware drinking cups decorated with hunting scenes. Over sixty vessels are represented in sherds of lustrous Rhenish ware.

Fig 8 Rhenish ware beakers from Lullingstone, Kent

Someone, possibly the owner of the villa himself, lost a carnelian intaglio and six coins in the house. The stone had been engraved with a winged Victory, wearing a sword and helmet and holding a shield, her left foot on a pile of stones. At some time the stone had been forced from its gold setting—a fracture on the reverse still contained fragments of metal.

The violence with which this ring was treated was perhaps a foretaste of the family fortunes. The idyllic life lasted not much more than a hundred years. The change was dramatic—the villa was totally abandoned and left to crumble. Belongings were left behind—the heirloom portraits left in the ruined house where they weathered to their present decayed state. What possible disaster could have struck this well-established family? The date suggested from the excavations is about the time of the struggle between Clodius Albinus and Septimius Severus (p 30). It could have been that the owner was one of the unlucky supporters of the usurper, so popular with the senatorial class, whose followers were punished so severely.

Whatever the fortunes of this family, the villa lay empty for almost a century, except for a tannery that was set up in the old kitchens.

Eventually new owners with enough money and the inclination to refurbish the house settled there. The arrangement of rooms did not suit their way of life. The pagan cult rooms were demolished, mosaic floors were added and a heated room was put in. In about 330 guests were feasting in a new dining-room. When reclining round the apse they could amuse themselves with a fine mosaic depicting the Rape of Europa. The border was a deep, rich red, the sea purple. Jupiter, having changed himself into a bull so that his dark deeds would not be discovered either by Europa or his consort Juno, is depicted galloping out of the sea with Europa on his back in a swirling cloak. Two cupids help him to take the lady to a fate worse than death. All the figures show up as would a pencil drawing, being mere outlines in red against the white background of the sky. Along the top was an elegiac couplet for the edification of the more educated guests:

INVIDA SI TA(uri) VIDISSET IVNO NATATVS
IVSTIVS AEOLIAS ISSET ADVSQVE DOMOS

('If jealous Juno had seen the swimming of the bull she would with greater justice on her side have repaired to the halls of Aeolus')

This rather obscure comment refers to Juno's plot to submerge Aeneas on a voyage, which, the writer of the couplet seemed to think, would have been a better fate for the faithless Jupiter.

The luxurious life at this villa came to an end dramatically with a fire in the early fifth century. The history of Lullingstone is illustrative of the changing fortunes that could be experienced in the most romanised of families. Even the idyllic existence that had come to be associated with the term 'villa' was transitory. Once the economic basis was lost, the villa was dead.

THE LAST VILLAS

What happened to villas at the end of the Roman period has long been in dispute. As with towns, no simple story fits all the establishments. Many whose prosperity depended on continental exports, on supplying the troops or on industry must have become obsolete or uneconomic units on the break-up of organised administration. Some, like Fishbourne, did not outlast the third century.

The indestructability of English life has always been remarkable, and the Roman period was no exception. This can easily be illustrated at Wharram Percy, which must be one of the most attractive corners of the British Isles. The fields rise steeply over the grassy valley sides, hiding the remains of a medieval village now long since dead. The church stands alone amid bluebell woods to show that this was once the home of English villagers. I went to the site when I was four. Not unnaturally the historical significance of the place was irrelevant to me. It was warm and balmy and we picked primroses. The pigeons who had made their home in the ruined nave and tower are still uppermost in my mind. It was entirely deserted except for my father and me, a place of enchantment and mystery. These characteristics still adhere to it, though twenty-five years of excavation on the deserted village have inevitably spoiled the air of undisturbed antiquity. Within recent years the excavators have been surprised to find a Romano-British farmhouse under the medieval layers. Not a luxury home but a viable economic unit which like so many in the Wolds had been amalgamated with neighbouring farms. Life at Wharram Percy at least was not destroyed for ever at the end of the Roman period.

4 Life in the Towns

In 1811 the Rev John Hodgson was at Chesterholm in North-umberland and saw the smoke-blackened pillars of the baths at the Roman fort, now more famous under its original name of Vindolanda. Local tradition claimed that the remains were the kitchen of a fairy queen's underground palace. Such was scientific deduction that the presence of the soot itself was deemed proof.

A VICUS

In the 1970s anyone can go to Vindolanda and see one of the most fascinating sites in Britain being slowly uncovered by archaeologists. Outside the fort was a fine example of one of the most lowly of Roman towns—a *vicus*. It was a modest settlement, but shared certain features in common with the tribal capitals, the colonies of veterans and the one *municipium* of Verulamium. The public baths so important in any town were in this case shared by the soldiers of the fort with the tinkers and pedlars, tradesmen, officials and their families. The inn already described (p 15) was faced by the largest house so far discovered; a series of six rooms arranged along a corridor in a common plan. Up to sixteen families could have been accommodated in the married quarters that must have become increasingly popular in the Empire after the third century when soldiers were allowed to marry for the first time. Many new recruits were found simply from the offspring of the original soldiery. Faced

Fig 9 Lady's slipper from Vindolanda

with a life of uncertainty and cattle rustling, many a British girl living near Vindolanda must have felt the rewards outweighed the problems of learning to wear Roman clothes or lead-based make-up. The original soldiers at this and other forts, with intriguing foreign accents and swarthy complexions could recount tales of battles on distant shores, and Roman coins could pay for such luxuries as perfume bottles or the elegant lady's slipper made by Lucius Aebutius Thales some time before AD 105.

TRIBAL CAPITALS

The tribal capitals (*civitas* capitals) were towns founded by Rome for the resettlement of Britons who had been dispossessed of their traditional and easily defended hillfort headquarters. They were self-governing and had a more classical outlook than the vici. No doubt life continued in tribal towns much as it had done before the conquest—though the local chief might have worn a toga and possibly aspired to owning a villa nearby. These were the equivalent of county towns—and only Silchester and Wroxeter have not been extensively obliterated by later buildings.

Wroxeter, in the heart of rural Shropshire, was originally a fortress of the fourteenth legion. When the legionary base was moved to Chester the Cornovii tribe were established in the new town. The town walls can be traced as slight bumps and hollows in the surrounding fields and the site is continuously under excavation. The original tribal hillfort of the Wrekin glowers over the town and the nearby Anglo-Saxon church of St Andrew incorporates Roman masonry. The most prominent feature of the town is the huge pockmarked lump of masonry known as the 'Old Work' which was once the entrance to the gymnasium of the public baths. These were extensive and included a suite of *laconica*, literally Spartan baths. The victim of the rigorous treatment apparently enjoyed the extreme dry heat. Once the limbering-up preliminaries were over the Romano-Briton could indulge in a more leisurely afternoon in the warm, hot and cold rooms with their plunge baths, or perhaps go for a dip in the swimming pool nearby.

In the new town the Romano-Britons learned to live in stone-built houses with separate rooms for eating, sleeping and entertaining guests. Water was brought by aqueduct and a complex system of drainage was installed.

THE MUNICIPIUM

Verulamium, like many towns, had military origins. The small fort was abandoned in AD 50 when the town was laid out. The remains of some of the earliest town buildings in Britain were discovered in excavations—charred and burnt relics of the massacre by Boudicca. What makes the town unique in Britain is its status as a *municipium*—effectively a city state in which the magistrates were given citizenship. As in other towns of

Fig 10 Dolphin and horse from St Albans

lesser prestige, the timber buildings were replaced in stone in the second century, and a wall was erected about a century later enclosing the settlement. This has not entirely perished, though very little masonry survives to any height. This is due to extensive stone robbing; there are records of the monks of St Albans taking the Roman remains to build their abbey. The stone robbing continued down to the eighteenth century. Stukeley records that

> out of wretched ignorance, even of their own interest, they have been pulling it up all around, to the very foundations, to mend the highway, and I met hundreds of cart loads of Roman bricks etc. carrying for that purpose.

COLONIAE

Colchester was the first British town. It was a legionary fortress which, when the troops moved to Lincoln in AD 47 was granted rights as a *colonia*, a model classical town that housed retired veterans. It is bound up almost inextricably with one of the most famous women in British history, Boudicca (Boadicea), the queen of the Norfolk tribe of the Iceni. What should have been a simple story of the foundation of a town turned out to be a tangled saga. In 61 king Prasutagus died, leaving half his estate to Rome, in the hope that his daughters would be allowed to retain the rest. Roman officials then looted his house, ill-treated his family and finally caused the Iceni under Boudicca to rebel, ambushing and massacring part of the ninth legion. The governor, Paulinus, who was campaigning in Anglesey in what turned out to be the final stages of the struggle against the druids, rushed back. The distance was too great to stop the rebellion and the towns of London, Colchester and St Albans were devastated, with 70,000 inhabitants reported dead. This ferocity and brutality was matched only by the Roman reprisal. A final battle took place in which the acting commander of the second legion refused to send help. On hearing that 80,000 Britons had been killed during the fight, he fell on his sword.

All record of this event was lost except in the pages of history books until archaeologists began excavating in Colchester. In 1927 blackened samian pots, stacked together ready for sale, were found along with molten pieces of glass vessels which had fused into them when flames swept through the city. Most poignant of all were the little heaps of charred corn found in 1964 within the original fort. These had once been supplied in sacks which, like the aged legionaries, had been destroyed through the fury of Boudicca.

The sack of Colchester can be discovered in the pages of Tacitus who describes how a reflection of the colonia in ruins had been seen in the Thames estuary, how the sea had been blood-red and how the spectre of corpses had appeared on the shore as the tide went out. His picture is a vivid evocation of impending doom, and above the cries of distraught women we can hear the crash of the statue of Victory collapsing in the city, its back to the enemy, as though in headlong flight.

The Romans however had sustained worse defeats than this, and the town was rebuilt along more splendid lines. Little remains above ground, except for the circuit of the town walls which were extensively repaired in medieval times. Two gates are still visible. Of these the Balkerne Gate vies with Lincoln's Newport Arch as one of the best preserved in Britain—one of the pedestrian arches and the adjacent guard-chamber survive intact.

One famous object associated with Colchester is now in the British Museum. It is a bronze head of the emperor Claudius, discovered in the river Alde. Possibly it had been torn from the body of its statue and found its way from the temple of Claudius at Colchester, carried as triumphant booty by some Icenian. Macabre without the eye insets it gazes at objects which Claudius would not himself have recognised and would have thought an odd collection to represent the way of life that he led. Museums, after all, can collect merely those objects which survive. Thus a case might contain such an ill assortment of objects as a pair of bronze shears for ritual castration, an ink pot with unspillable lip, and perhaps priceless pieces of jewellery.

EVERYDAY LIFE IN TOWNS

The forum was the most important feature of any town. Here business could be discussed, traders could proffer their wares, leaders could address the people and young boys gathered round their mentors from dawn till dusk without even a break for lunch. Here the merchants would have brought their wares— silk from the East, and occasionally a batch of cotton, linen and woollen clothes of all weights in sea green, saffron (the colour traditionally worn by brides) and red; a splendid array of colours to adorn British womenfolk. Hair-pieces of black locks from Indian girls or blonde tresses from German slaves might have been available to improve on nature. The hair was fixed on to a piece of leather, and one firm in Mainz actually specialised in bleaching hair-pieces, suggesting that gentlemen have always preferred blondes. From the few clues afforded by represent- ations it seems that British womenfolk were not behind in hair fashion, though it probably took several years for some styles to reach this island from Rome.

The toga, that hallmark of civilisation, was paradoxically going out of fashion in Rome when it was adopted enthusiastic- ally in the provinces. Several emperors had actually decreed that the garment should only be worn on formal occasions. Men, who had previously worn the traditional Celtic trousers would have struggled with the 13ft of woollen folds. To go with the new tunics and togas the young warrior aspiring to be a noble Roman would have had to have a haircut. Barbers' shops abounded in towns, uncannily like modern hairdressers, where

Plate 5 The Roman theatre at Verulamium (St Albans). *(author)*

Plate 6 Verulamium (St Albans), Hertfordshire. A section of wall at the south of the site, with a corner tower clearly visible. *(John Bethell)*

Plate 7 (left) The finest visor helmet yet to be found in Britain, discovered at Ribchester, Lancashire. Dated late first century AD, it is made of bronze. *(British Museum)*

Plate 8 (below) A leather sandal from Newstead, Scotland. *(National Museum of Antiquities of Scotland)*

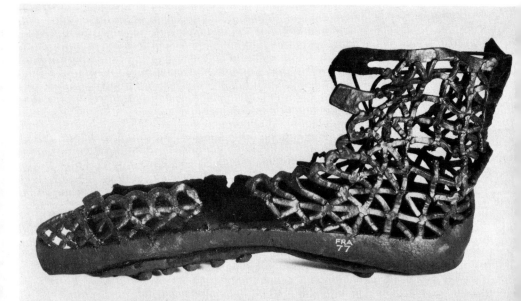

the customers waited their turn on benches before being swathed in a large wrap and having their beards shaved excruciatingly without soap with razors like the fearsome example from Lockleys villa. No doubt in Britain togas fell into disfavour along with shaving. When the emperor Hadrian discarded tradition and grew a beard, the Empire, thankfully, followed suit.

The best place (in 1976) to discover the everyday life of Roman town dwellers is probably in the Corinium Museum in

Fig 11   Reconstruction of the interior of a Roman dining-room based on a model in the Corinium Museum, Chichester

Cirencester. Here the rooms have been arranged 'as they would have appeared to a Roman', complete with models dressed in reproduction Roman clothes. The similarities between the standards of living in the rich household depicted and those of later centuries are very marked. An urbane person of almost any age would have had few complaints if shown into a room with such elegant couches and low tables set with fruits imported from almost as many countries as today. If Roman floors lacked wall-to-wall carpets, they had more labour-saving mosaics.

The walls were painted lavishly and with colours imitated

and made famous in eighteenth-century England. Many an Adam house has more than a little of the atmosphere of a great Roman mansion. The lack of windows in Roman houses meant that wall coverings had to be spectacular to avoid claustrophobia. There is little reason to doubt that Romano-British houses were well-painted. Fragments of garden and bird scenes from Fishbourne and St Albans, now in the site museum and the British Museum respectively, illustrate the taste of the time. The Verulamium frescoes included pictures of candelabra with garlands, which were popular from Pompeii to Trier. Some scenes are more ambitious—among fragments of frescoes found in Roman London are Bacchic orgies and the god Mercury. A remarkable series of walls painted in bright colours were discovered during excavations at Dover in 1973.

While some aspects of Roman life, such as religion or warfare, are difficult for the modern Briton to comprehend, the culinary arts were basically similiar. An open slab over the reconstructed museum oven recalls ceramic hobs. The shelves are festooned with herbs and vegetables, game hangs from hooks, and pots are ready for use. Bronze cooking vessels stood on gridles, and the *paterae* (saucepans) could be used today. The food produced was often rich and bizarre to modern tastes. We are fortunate in that the recipe book of Apicius, a first-century Robert Carrier, survives, and from it we can see that he at any rate favoured exotic sauces. His recipes tell how to cook such delicacies as ostrich, and suggest up to fifteen ways of cooking more common fowl. Rotten-fish sauce was apparently popular, or, if the finer foods were beyond the purse, there was always unleavened bread, eggs, fruit and humbler stews.

In a triangular corner of the museum complex, open to the sky, an imaginative planner has built a Roman *impluvium*, the open area in the centre of a Roman town house, in which herbs familiar to the Romans now grow. Corinium Museum is a far cry from museums such as those on Hadrian's Wall, where the finds are displayed in timber huts not unlike the barrack buildings of the first Roman forts themselves.

ENTERTAINMENT

As I followed the A48 to Caerwent one Saturday evening, the Chepstow races were just ending: people of all ages swarmed across the road like the population of a Roman town after a day at the Cursus (racecourse). No Roman racecourse has yet been found in Britain, but fairly common places of entertainment are amphitheatres, which are found outside both forts and towns. One such can be seen outside Dorchester, Dorset. Here until the eighteenth century public hangings were conducted— a fitting place, perhaps, where slaughter of both animals and humans must have taken place during the Roman period. Certainly gladiators and touring circuses went round Britain, and from Dorchester they might have gone on to the very cosmopolitan tribal capital of Petuaria (Brough-on-Humber) which though smaller than any other capital (a mere thirteen acres) was a model of its kind and boasted a fine arena. In the Dorchester amphitheatre, which is known as Maumbury Rings, the Romans lowered the ground level and blocked up one of the two opposing entrances of a neolithic henge before setting up tiers of wooden seats. It was in use probably from the second to the fourth century. Today the sports taking place in it are contributing to its ruin. Children slide on sledges made out of cardboard boxes down the 30ft of its banks where once sat the cheering populace of Durnorvaria. They tumble into the arena floor in giggling, screaming heaps, watched by the not infrequent visitors from the crest of the bank.

Less blood-thirsty entertainment could be found in the theatres. Of these an outstanding example can be seen at Verulamium (St Albans). Built in the middle of the second century, when it was probably used for religious ceremonies, it was enlarged in the latter part of the century and again in the fourth, presumably due to its popularity. The theatre is typical of classical theatres everywhere, the descendant of those at Epidauros, Delphi and Athens. The stage was originally used as a dance floor in the Greek theatre, but at Verulamium may have had other functions. A wooden pole stood in the centre, possibly as a stake for animals in blood sports. Round the orchestra, which was entered by three gaps, were tiers of seats as in an amphitheatre.

5 The Fighting Force

Forts tell the story of those Britons who were not acquiescent to Rome if promises and titles had little effect: the substantially built military foundations have withstood weathering and stone robbing. Walls could be 10ft thick, faced with smoothly dressed stones on a rubble core, surrounded by up to seven ditches and backed up by ballista-fire and highly trained soldiery. Like all the Celts, the Britons were more used to settling quarrels by guerilla tactics or by tribal champions, with little loss of blood. They were not easily overcome by the organisation of Roman armies. It was not until the boundaries of the Empire had been overstretched that Rome began to take on a defensive position.

The Roman historian Suetonius gives a dispassionate account of spectacular defeats in southern Britain. During the initial conquest the commander (later emperor) Vespasian had little trouble in demolishing the hillforts with their complicated ramparts. Of those Britons who died or were wounded defending their way of life and their freedom, there is little trace in the Roman history books, except in passing as the agency of triumphs for particular commanders. Their pathetic struggles turn up in excavations—the most famous are those skeletons, with the weapons of death embedded in the bones, found at Maiden Castle, Dorset.

The Britons, like all barbarians, lacked organisation. Hod Hill, Dorset, is idyllic on a sunny day, commanding a wide view

Fig 12   Cheek-piece of a bronze helmet from South Shields

of the countryside. It seems astonishing that the Romans had such success in demolishing the vast defences. Hod is remarkable for, amongst other things, having a Roman fort incorporated into its defences. Utilising one corner, the Romans added two more sides to form a rectangle within which they built their barracks.

MILITARY REMAINS

Roman forts are always much smaller than British hillforts. The Iron Age Britons had no army—in the event of war, it seems that all able-bodied people helped. Raiding and cattle rustling were far greater problems than enemy invaders, so hillforts with ramparts enclosing hundreds of acres were the obvious method of keeping humans and animals safe. Roman civilisation depended on a more aggressive policy. The army was highly efficient. The cream of the fighting force—the legions—were citizens, and their fortresses were impressive. Examples in Britain were built at Caerleon, Chester, York, Exeter, Gloucester, Lincoln, Wroxeter and Inchtuthil, though the first three were the final headquarters. Less prestigious were the auxiliaries who were recruited from newly conquered lands. In 212 (or 214) the emperor Caracalla extended the citizenship to all those living within the Empire's bounds, and the distinction between legionaries and auxiliaries was less clear-cut. From the third century Britain was host to new troops called *numeri*, who were less established, raw barbarians, called to fight for Rome.

Legionaries were always given headquarters in safe areas, shielded by a network of auxiliary forts. Agricola once boasted that the battle of Mons Graupius (somewhere in Scotland) was won without the loss of Roman blood. This simply meant that the only casualties were the non-citizen auxiliaries. If the superstition I was taught as a child is true, legionaries must have suffered frequently—'aconites grow only where Roman blood was spilled'.

Fig 13 The Newport Arch, Lincoln

59

All fortresses were built to a similar plan—a rectangle with rounded corners of fifty acres or so to accommodate between 5,000 and 6,000 men. Auxiliary forts are smaller but similar in plan. Inside were the barracks, workshops and stores, the head-quarters building and commandant's house. Generally the bath buildings were outside the walls, to minimise the risk of fire from the furnaces. As expediencies and fashion changed, differences in gateways and defences can be detected.

Marching camps were put up at the end of a day's march. They are temporary structures: simple banks and ditches topped originally by a timber fence. These are usually seen only either from the air or from a long distance; those round the Scottish Highlands are particularly remarkable.

Also temporary were practice camps, usually found in groups as a result of army manoeuvres. Various other military remains such as signal stations and siege works are visible in the same areas.

In the National Museum of Wales is a collection of buff-orange pottery made at the military workshops at Holt, Flint-shire. As might be expected of utility ware produced for army use, it is undecorated and unglazed. But the execution of the simple forms is so competent, each rim and body finished off to such a high degree, that they must rank amongst the finest works of pottery ever produced in the British Isles.

The workmanship displayed in military remains reflects the high organisation and skill of the soldiers who lived in them. Some of the finest works of art in inscriptions, in pictorial reliefs, in pottery and metalwork were made by the army. The soldiers were expected not merely to be good fighters, but to specialise in carpentry, masonry, smithing, or baking—whatever was required to run the regiments.

By AD 47 the south of Britain had been subdued; a frontier along the Fosse Way was studded with timber forts which have long since perished. By AD 80 Wales had been added to the province and Scotland had been explored as far as Banff (to judge from the line of temporary marching camps visible from the air). The frontier was established along the Stanegate, a road between Solway and Tyne, by 105. This line was made more concrete by the construction of Hadrian's Wall and later in the second century the Antonine Wall (p 74). By this time, those military establishments that were to be garrisoned permanently were rebuilt in stone.

ENGLAND

I first became familiar with the legionary fortress of Chester one Christmas-time. The excavations in the principia, the headquarters building and focal point of the great fortress that held the key routes into Scotland and Wales, were underway. The snow and ice were so severe that the first task was to remove about 10in of snow and ice from the frozen excavations in order to reveal the previous week's work. It was not at all as I had expected an excavation to be. Out of the sides of the cutting projected medieval Britain—the remains of the thriving town that had been founded on the site of the Roman fort around 907 by the Saxon queen Ethelflaeda.

At the end of the morning the trench looked more respectable and the finds tray appreciably fuller with bits of pottery and the odd stones that I had in ignorance collected. Somehow it all seemed very dirty and unspectacular, though from later experience I realise it was amazingly eventful compared with the day to day events of most excavations. A weird shape appeared in the side of the trench—a rounded piece of dull grey-brown pottery that looked like a modern drainpipe. Tentatively I prodded it with my trowel and was caught before I did any damage by the director who overlooked my lack of archaeological principle and explained that this uninspiring object was the mouth of an amphora. Never again did I prod objects from excavations with a trowel. It seemed incredible that this dirty piece of pottery could have been lost some time between the establishment of the fortress in 76–9 by the Second Adiutrix legion, and the change of garrison in 87 when the Twentieth Valeria Victrix replaced it. The wine container had lain underground through all the changes of policy and loyalties in the third century, through the destruction of the fort some time in the latter part of that century, and through the last rebuilding in the early fourth century. When the final abandonment came the legions of Rome left Deva to its decay, the amphora lay undisturbed until my trowel so nearly destroyed it, 1,588 years later.

From 105 onwards, Chester was of an importance paralleled only by York or Caerleon. Of this greatness, surprisingly extensive remains can be seen. In the stretch of the city wall just north of the Eastgate, for instance, the masonry stands 15ft high. Other stretches are more difficult to see, as the walls of the fort have been rebuilt above the first few courses by the medieval fabricators of the city wall.

The largest military amphitheatre in Britain lies uneasily bordered by the main ring route, which makes a deliberate detour round its edge. Only half of this arena has escaped being submerged by the nearby convent. But, while several arenas in Britain are romantically grassed over or even downright overgrown, that at Chester, with its gravelled interior and substantial masonry walls, is military and classical in its impressiveness. West of one entrance lies the shrine of Nemesis, the goddess of Fate, a sharp reminder that this semi-circle, now a pleasant place for sunbathing, with the benches overlooking it almost as a public park, was the scene of violent death for both animals and humans. It is difficult to credit, with the car park, garages, pedestrian ways, traffic lights, fire station, police and other life-saving methods available in Chester, amid the innocence of afternoon shoppers stopping for tea in a café, that some 1,676 years ago the course of one man's life had reached such a crisis that a dedication was made to the goddess of Fate. Indeed, it is almost certain that two such pleas for life were made, though now only the column bases of the monuments which probably carried the invocations survive. From the arena of another legionary fortress, Caerleon, a curse has come engraved on a piece of lead damning a fellow competitor or gladiator. It reads 'Lady Vengeance, I give these cloak and shoes. Let him who wore them not redeem them unless by the life of his chestnut horse.' That is, the curse calls for the death of the rival unless his steed dies first. The most common use for amphitheatres outside forts was not for shows but simply for the practice of hand-to-hand combat.

There are less spectacular sides to Chester. Browsing through the gown shop of Nola Ltd, in Northgate Row, with its exterior covered arcade, the fashionable woman might be forgiven for not having Romans on her mind. Yet underneath this shop, in the cellar incongruously piled with boxes and other back-of-the-counter paraphernalia, are the giant columns that once supported the headquarters building or principia. The masonry is colossal in such an enclosed space, but it is not too impossible to imagine Magnus Maximus leaning against them as he exhorted the local commanders to cross the Channel and fight for independence. All usurpers must have travelled the countryside extensively in those days when power lay not in votes, nor in the impression made on the media, but in personal involvement and leadership of the army.

Legionaries could not be expected to share the accommodation of lesser soldiers. Hod Hill is one of the few forts built for both types of military personnel. Auxiliary forts are infinitely more numerous and differ from legionary establishments in size and details only. High in the Langdale mountains of Cumbria the fourth cohort of Dalmatians was stationed at Hardknott Castle from the time of Hadrian (AD 117–38) until the end of that century when only a small caretaker force was left. In this enclosure the Yugoslavian troops waited for the attack that seems never to have come, although they were well within the territory of the Brigantes. Outside the walls is the flattened area of the parade ground.

Today, the fort's position is breathtaking, especially if approached across the pass. I once arrived there driving an ancient Mini crammed with archaeologists and their equipment, the car held in gear by the strength of the front seat passenger. The road winds perilously to the top, at times awash with streams from the hillside, and several times when I have visited it powerful cars have been seen precipitously parked as their owners, oblivious of the view, gathered their nerves to continue. A march across the terrain can plunge the adventurous tourist in the marsh if he strays from the official path. The fort can be terrifying—total isolation with the only movement being from the grey-black rain-laden clouds, or beautiful—a shimmering fairytale castle. Alas, even in this remote corner of Britain stone robbers or souvenir hunters have been at work and the hypocaust of the external bath-house found in the nineteenth century has now disappeared.

Any traveller who chanced to leave the motorway just south of Birmingham to meander for a change through some country lanes in 1967 might have seen an astonishing sight; prisoners cutting turves to the Roman dimensions on the site of a Roman fort and stacking them turf to turf in a bank. For three weeks they toiled, until their reproduction rampart was completed. Three years later, a group of Royal Engineers took on the challenge of building a Roman gateway on the site in a weekend.

In the first century this was a cavalry training centre, with the unusual feature of a *gyrus* where the horses were trained. By now the granaries of the fort have been rebuilt, using wood from trees struck down by the scourge of Dutch Elm disease. They are impressively sturdy, raised up above ground level on stilts which kept at bay both damp and rats, and eventually they will house the site museum.

WALES

In the '60s and '70s campaigns were focused on Wales and the North. The druids, whose powers to incite insurrection had caused the Romans much trouble on the continent, were finally cornered in Anglesey. While there were members of this priestly caste alive to fan the fires of native resistance, the conquest of Britain and Gaul would never be finalised. In the end, the druids were outwitted by the resource of the Roman commander Suetonius Paulinus. Arriving at the Menai Straits he ferried his infantry across the water in flat-bottomed boats, and despite their protests ordered the cavalry to swim their horses across. Such indignities were followed by an awesome spectacle—black-robed women with dishevelled hair brandished torches and a group of druids lifted up their hands and uttered frightful curses. The Romans were momentarily dismayed, but rallied under their strict training. The druids were overwhelmed, the sacred groves destroyed and Anglesey was garrisoned.

A stirring reminder of the last days of the druids in Anglesey came to light when a runway was being built on the island at Llyn Cerrig Bach during World War II. In the first century AD offerings had been thrown into a pool from a rock shelf. Because of the wartime demands only a fraction of the hoard was recovered, and the rest probably still lies buried, but even so the 138 objects now in the National Museum of Wales bring the Iron Age vividly to life. Apart from bones of ponies, oxen and sheep, parts of a chariot, swords, scabbards, daggers, gang chains for slaves, tongs, bracelets, spears with their ash wood shafts, two cauldrons, shields, decorative bronze mounts and parts of a trumpet were dredged up. When the haul was grubbed up out of the peat by the jaws of a mechanical excavator in 1943, one of the slave-gang chains was used to haul lorries out of the peat in which they had become bogged down before its age was realised.

The Roman occupation of Wales is exemplified by the remote auxiliary fort of Tomen-y-Mur. It is often regarded as one of the most unattractive of the Welsh outposts. High above the Merionethshire valley, the banks and ditches show up clearly from a distance. In the centre, the most prominent feature is the Norman motte, though the Roman stonework of the fort walls can be seen in parts. It is approached by a tortuous route through pinewoods, but I visited it several times in blazing sunshine and watched lambs play king of the castle on its ramparts. Without asking permission first, only the ludus is available to walk round. This is now a bank around a flat marshy area where troops once practised hand-to-hand combat.

Many forts in Wales were never rebuilt in stone, presumably as there was little need to man them when the frontier was moved to Hadrian's Wall. Accordingly many are almost invisible except as changes in vegetation colour. They are worth searching for, with the help of OS maps, often being in particularly scenic areas. Many such remains were never meant to last—Roman military camps for instance were temporary establishments, used for a night or so at a time. Some were apparently put up, not by the army on the march but during manoeuvres, and can sometimes occur in groups.

The main Welsh legionary fortress of Caerleon is now a small settlement whose winding streets have forced traffic into a one-way system. The history of Caerleon has included the building of a Norman motte and the romantically overgrown bastion near the river belongs to this phase. In the centre of the village stands a splendid classically inspired temple. Not the place of worship of some pagan deity but literally a temple of the Muses, the custodians of the arts. The antiquarianism is deliberate, for after conducting excavations on the fortress in 1849, John

Edward Lee had this museum built to house his finds at a cost of £250.

Caerleon is essentially a military foundation. It was the most important establishment in Wales, the home of the Second Augustan legion from 74–5 until the end of the third century. Accordingly it is fitting that on entering the museum, the visitor's attention should be arrested by a lifesize model of a soldier. His piercing gaze, the bright red tunic and scarf under shiny body armour, put one in no doubt as to the inadvisability of defying Roman legionaries. In his hand is a fiercesome missile spear, with a long shank cunningly designed to bend on impact to prevent its being thrown back by the enemy. Tiny fragments of armour and various weapons in the museum further proclaim the presence of the army.

The fortress itself is unexposed except for a large section of barrack blocks in the NW corner. The low walls, tastefully consolidated in pink mortar, are arranged according to the Roman plan in rows. Only the outlines are visible, regimented and orderly. In the centre stood the headquarters block from which came a fine stone slab in low relief. Found, fittingly under the police station in 1865, it shows a mastiff baiting a bear, and is an indication of the quality of the headquarters furniture. In one museum case is a bronze leaf, once used as a stop in some monumental inscription. Only the very best work would have necessitated such an object being embedded in the stone.

The military aspect of the site was completed in Spring 1976, by a coachload of army cadets, less colourfully attired than their Roman counterparts, but orderly under the supervision of an officer and instructor. They filed round the barrack blocks, no doubt listening to the disadvantages and advantages of Roman fort planning like any potential recruits at the very same fortress nearly 2,000 years before under the wing of a centurion. The defences are plainly visible—a wall with typically straight sides is exposed for a short stretch—including the rounded corners, but disappears under a grassy bank. Under long wild grass the ramparts and ditches are clearly visible, following the wall circuit.

The lighter side of life at Caerleon leaves traces in the museum cases. A glass phial contains charred grain—spelt, wheat, barley and rye. The presence of Mediterranean weeds suggests that this was beer being malted at a stage of brewing. Possibly some kind of do-it-yourself brew kit. It is interesting to note that hops were not used to flavour beer (*carvesia*) at this time.

The popularity of the drink would have been apparent during carousals and celebrations. Wine, of course was consumed—a wine jug from Caerleon is scratched with the words 'Good luck to the presiding spirit of the Century of Aelius Romulus'—this was perhaps a relic of a second-century regimental dinner.

All this intoxicating liquor would have been soaked up in bread baked in the company ovens. Leaden dies in the museum include one with the words 'Century of Vibius Severus (produced by) Sentius Paulinus'. Bread was an important part of the Roman diet. Along the fortress walls near the barracks are round ovens, some visible as stone slabs, others as bumps in the turf. An unusual portable military oven is displayed in the National Museum of Wales. It is barrel-shaped, in an attractive orange pottery and decorated with a simple pie-crust effect. The bread was lowered in from the top, and the ashes raked out at the bottom through a stoke hole.

Without a doubt the most impressive structure at Caerleon is the amphitheatre, just outside the fort. Its enclosed circuit is echoed by the distant hills. The walls are softened by well-manicured banks on top with wilder grass and plants spilling down over the masonry. Like the fort, this has been consolidated in an incongruous bathroom-pink mortar, but the masonry is monumental and unmistakably legionary work. On the north side pink-red bricks complement the buff stones of a shrine,

Plate 9 Silver *antoninianus* of Philip I (AD 244–49) from the Dorchester hoard, Dorset, found in 1936. This was probably part of the tax collection for Durnovaria. The reverse shows the Emperor on horseback. Scale 2 × 1. *(Author)*

Plate 10 Official coin of Constantine II and British imitations of the fourth century. 'Soldier spearing fallen horseman' type. *(Author)*

Plate 11 A shrine in the amphitheatre at Caerleon, Gwent. *(John Bethell)*

Plate 12 Hardknott Castle, a Roman fort in Northumbria. *(Aerofilms Library)*

probably to Nemesis, with an arched niche for an altar or a statue. It is easy standing in the centre of this powerful arena to understand how it could have become associated in popular imagination with the legendary King Arthur. It has even been suggested that this was the original Round Table.

Caerleon is rivalled in the north by the auxiliary fort at Segontium, now Caernarvon. The site boasts two forts, one enclosing the car park of the Department of Social Security with walls standing twenty feet high. This belongs to a series of forts built in the third century and later apparently to repel barbarian invaders. Nine lie along the eastern and southern coasts, and Cardiff and Lancaster complete the scheme. Those of the 'Saxon Shore' are mysterious and often overpowering remains. Lympne, the first fort I ever tried to find (p 7) is one of them. They belong to a period when history is confused, and several even seem to have been built during the short reign of Carausius. It has been suggested that they were built to repel not barbarians, but the orthodox armies of Rome come to reclaim the province. It seems amazing that excavations have not yet produced enough evidence, as with Hadrian's Wall, to prove or disprove any one theory. Whatever was in the official mind, the forts were well placed to deal with danger from without.

Pevensey Saxon Shore fort is an outstanding example of British economy drives. A casual glance round the ruins reveals a Norman castle with its keep. A closer scrutiny of the curtain wall shows that some of the 'bastions' are World War II pill-boxes. The lower portions of the walls are Roman. The castle is the response to the few occasions in the last two thousand years when Britain has been in most peril from violent attack.

Portchester is arguably the best Saxon Shore fort, but its forbidding walls can be claustrophobic. The circuit is almost intact, but was refaced by the Normans in parts. The wall-walk

E
71

is original, and was patrolled by Roman sentries and medieval soldiers alike. Richborough too is preserved to a remarkable degree. It is approached by a winding lane through Kentish fields, and the 20ft high walls are discovered by surprise. The site was occupied throughout the Roman period. The island (as it was then) in the Wantsum was used as a base in the Claudian invasion, and later the site became a supply base for the troops as they pushed north. A marble-encased monument was erected, probably to commemorate the conquest, in about AD 85, and is still visible as a vast cruciform concrete foundation. It was eventually re-used as a watch tower. There are remains of successive forts, but the flint and mortar circuit so impressive today belongs to the Saxon Shore phase. There is evidence to connect Carausius with this fort, and it may be that it was on his orders that the earthen fort was infilled and these huge walls and bastions erected. So strong is Roman mortar that in places where the walls have not withstood weathering, they have fallen in large sections, rather than crumbling slowly.

Few Roman remains are more peaceful that the Saxon Shore fort at Burgh Castle in Norfolk. There is less to be seen than in the others, and much of the walls have collapsed into massive lumps of mortar, flints and tiles, but many people have been attracted to Burgh. The fields around, the mellowness of the walls that have come to terms with their environment, the now distant sea, the broken bastions, the warm silence that only summer birds and insects can produce make it an antiquary's paradise. Here Saint Fursa came in the seventh century and spent ten years before leaving for the Continent; remains of what may be his monastery have been found in excavations within the fort, which was given to him by the king. The sea has eroded one side, and the Normans built a motte in one corner. Corn grows within the shelter of the fort, and civilisation seems far away.

The walls stand 15ft high and 8ft thick, massively built with lines of tiles at every few courses; the most typical method of Roman building. The bastions are simple enough, until closely inspected. They are not bonded in at the bottom, but at the top and are of one build with the walls. They are massive indeed, not hollowed out but infilled. They face the seaward side; infiltrating barbarians would first have seen these vast walls of the fort. On top of the bastions almost certainly stood hefty ballistae—spaced too closely together, however, for effective fire. The fort was designed at a period when, apparently, Rome felt it necessary to impress outsiders with a show of strength as well as actual physical force.

6 The Edge of Civilisation

At Birdoswald in Spring, the crisp fields make urbanised minds stop and consider whether the ancient Greeks were right to assert that cities were the pinnacle of civilised achievement. At Birdoswald a farm peaceably produces lambs every year within the safety of 6ft wide Roman fort walls. These massive stones and mortar, tied as they are to the great frontier of Hadrian's Wall, emphasise the lengths to which the Roman Empire went to keep civilisation and its values intact. In about AD 122, when the Stanegate frontier was still relatively new, a decision was made that only a Roman emperor could have conceived. The Brigantes were still enjoying too much success, allied to the Novantae and Selgovae in the north. Logically, coldly and ambitiously it was decided to cut them off from their friends, by building a wall from sea to sea. So great was the haste to complete this massive undertaking of seventy-eight miles, that where natural stone was scarce a turf wall was improvised. This, in the fullness of time, was replaced in stone. At Birdoswald the temporary turf wall and its more durable successor are both visible.

It seems incredible that, using only hand tools, a wall 10ft high and up to 10ft wide with a surmounting parapet should have been erected by legionaries in six to eight years. Along the structure were full-scale forts, with all the necessary internal and external buildings. A small castle marked every Roman mile and between the castles two turrets looked out over the countryside.

74

Along the Solway coast military establishments counteracted infiltration by sea. Roman boundaries traditionally followed natural land barriers. The Solway and Tyne estuaries, roughly linked by that tremendous basalt outcrop known as the Whin Sill was obviously the most sensible place from an engineering and geographical standpoint to build the limit of the Empire. Sadly for the Romans, tribal territory was not so easily demarcated. The Wall not only severed the Brigantes from their northern allies but divided the tribe itself; the northern branch was a constant threat. To the south at Stanwix was a fort for an *ala miliaria*—a specialist regiment of crack fighters which were placed only in positions of great danger. No others of this type are known in Britain, and the commander was senior to those in the Wall forts. From Stanwix the commander could communicate with the legionary headquarters at York within a few minutes through signal stations. One such signal tower at Pike Hill on the Wall commands a wide view of North Cumbria, facing the watch tower at Gillalees and the signal station at Walltown Crags. It has extra deep foundations, probably to support additional height for fast long-distance signalling. When I visited the signal tower in 1976 I walked back along the line of the Wall to the next turret. Here in the shadow of the grey walls I came across the empty containers of someone's emergency food supply. It was marked 'Provisions Pack A' and had instructions on it explaining how to prepare the victuals inside if stranded on some lonely mountain top. I don't know whether it was left by a soldier or an unusually well-equipped hiker, but no doubt the Roman commissariat would have issued similar 'life support systems' to the soldiers patrolling these inhospitable hills.

Life on the Wall was lonely and tense for the ordinary soldier. Many insurrections have left their mark in the burnt layers of excavations, and the inscriptions put up in rebuilt forts, tell a grim tale of fire and devastation. Since insurrection was as likely to come from the south as the north, the Wall was merely part of a wide military zone delimited in the north by a ditch and turf revetted banks and separated from the Wall by a 30ft berm. On the south the ditch is called the *Vallum*, and was continuous except where causeways allowed official access at forts and some milecastles.

Whereas the ditch in the north occasionally disappears in the south no rock was deemed too tough, and its course was rigorously adhered to, despite the hardships. Nowhere can this be seen more clearly than at Limestone Corner, which despite its name is an outcrop of particularly tough basalt. Here the line of the Vallum is like some lunar landscape, with huge boulders of rock strewn along its course as though some vast machine had just ploughed a furrow. But each block has been hewn from the living rock with wedges, and heaved up with only the simplest of equipment. The fact that it was deemed essential to cut the ditch at this point shows that it had a symbolic significance beyond that of defence. There was absolutely no doubt where the limits of the Empire lay, and any unauthorised Briton caught in the military zone would have had difficulty in escaping unscathed.

RECRUITMENT

Hadrian's Wall is the place to look for the remains of the widest cross-section of Romano-British population. In this border country lived men of differing ranks, origins, trades and religions, united only in the cause of fighting for civilisation. Even among the natives there were those whose sympathies lay with Rome, and those who fought on relentlessly. Massacres or attacks could be followed by peaceful trading or the encouragement of agriculture. Commands might come to sally forth and put down an uprising, to demolish an obsolete fort, to refurbish another, or to withdraw to the south. If life was for long periods uneventful, in the space of two and a half centuries

Hadrian's Wall saw a wide panorama of human endeavour and folly.

Most of the frontier troops were recruited elsewhere, but men were drafted from nearer home. Many Roman regiments with exotic names such as the First Cohort of the Batavians or First Cohort of Cugernians (who came from Germany), both of whom served at Carrawburgh, would have consisted of men primarily of British origin, no doubt with foreign blood some generations back. In the early days the outlook of the auxiliaries recently recruited from barbarian border peoples would have differed little from their enemies across the Wall. When in the third century *numeri* were enlisted further barbarians were paid to fight in the name of Rome. Surely one of the most extraordinary feats of the Empire was to persuade barbarian to fight barbarian in the name of civilisation.

THE WALL AND ARCHAEOLOGY

Hadrian's Wall has been the focus of enlightened interest since as long ago as the eighth century when the Venerable Bede wrote about it in the following terms, believing it to be the work of Septimius Severus:

After many crucial and hotly contested battles he [ie Severus] decided to separate the portion of the island under his jurisdiction from the remaining unconquered peoples, which he did not with a wall of stone as some believe but with an earthwork. For a wall is built of stone but an earthwork, like those that protect a camp from enemy attack, is constructed with turfs cut from the ground and raised high above ground level, fronted by a ditch from which the sods are cut, and surmounted by a strong palisade of logs. Severus built a rampart and ditch of this type from sea to sea, and fortified it with a series of towers.

Since then it has been tramped over by antiquaries, archaeo-

77

logists and walkers, and has been drawn and excavated, surveyed, theorised about and wondered at. It is therefore a little surprising that such an apparently simple question as 'When was the Wall occupied?' can lead to discussion, dissention and battles. The evidence is fragmentary and confusing, presumably a good mirror of life on the frontier. Garrisons were changed frequently, when troops were withdrawn to the Continent.

There is often little to distinguish archaeologically between a fort sacked by a native uprising and one deliberately demolished by the withdrawing troops. With so many excavations each year, many sites can boast to shedding new light on Hadrian's Wall and its sister the Antonine Wall. What seems certain is that Hadrian's Wall was built between about 122 and 128. Presumably further unrest among the Brigantes led Antoninus Pius in 139–40 to have the ditches filled in, the milecastle gates removed and a further wall between the Clyde and Forth isthmus built. Although more forts were packed into a mere thirty-eight miles this construction was less successful. If Hadrian's Wall was too far south, that of Antoninus Pius was too far north. By about 159–60 Hadrian's Wall had been occupied then depleted. Perplexingly a study of the pottery shows that this northern frontier was again in occupation in 163. It seems that Hadrian's Wall was first destroyed by enemy action in about 197 when Clodius Albinus took troops abroad—the British tribes were always well informed of political events in Rome and were very capable of taking advantage of them. The Wall was refurbished in about AD 205–8—a long time before its postulated destruction —which has led to suggestions that it was in fact destroyed around 203. During this reconstruction the Vallum was left obsolete, the gateways to the milecastles were narrowed (a defensive measure), and some suburbs outside forts spilled over the course of the Vallum. Septimius Severus supervised these changes himself, and campaigned against the Scottish tribes. Their guerilla tactics finally proved too much for him and the emperor died, worn out, in York in 211. His sons Geta and Caracalla, agreeing for once, made a peace and left the country to pursue their enmity to its logical conclusion. Murdered in his mother's arms by his brother, even references to Geta's name were erased in inscriptions.

A long peace apparently followed, doubtless interspersed with many a skirmish, until the Wall was destroyed in the time of Allectus, the murderer of Carausius. The man who defeated him, Constantius Chlorus, refurbished the Wall, but in 383 the natives prevailed once more during the bid for power by Magnus Maximus. A few people seem to have continued to live in the forts until the turn of the century, but effectively the frontier had been lost. Both Hadrian's and the Antonine Wall, arrogant feats of engineering, crumbled slowly through the centuries.

The best place to experience the Wall of the second century is to the south of its line, at Vindolanda, that much excavated and publicised fort on the Stanegate. Here a stretch of wall was reconstructed by staff and pupils provided by Gateshead Education Authority. A turf wall, topped by a timber palisade, timber milecastle and gateway, and a typical stone turret dominate the site. When I went there in 1976 the timbers smelt heathily of primer and mushrooms clung perilously to the bank. Although constructed in 1972 and 1974, within two years the reconstruction was beginning to look a little the worse for wear—the timber palisade leaned dangerously over the eroding rampart. Nevertheless it is a salutary experience to see this reconstruction.

Behind the reconstruction of the Wall and its crenellated gateway and milecastle, stands a fierce-looking ballista ready to repel any attacker. These giant catapults had remarkable force. During lectures, the late Dr Eric Marsden frequently used to fire an orange with astonishing accuracy from a model ballista through an open window, to the vocally expressed astonishment of passers-by. In Roman warfare the shot was more lethal. Many

79

museums, especially in military areas, contain the stone balls and iron bolts or arrows fired from them—their effective killing range was up to 400 yards. In the museum at Vindolanda, too, can be seen reconstructions of Celtic and Roman chariots, life-size, which look like abandoned props for *Ben Hur*.

There are many lovely ruins along the line of Hadrian's Wall. Perhaps none is more picturesque than Chesters, where 500 Asturian horsemen made their base, according to the *Notitia Dignitatum*, an early fifth-century list of Imperial officials. Luck was with these soldiers from Spain when the fort was built: the land slopes gently down to the river Tyne. A Roman bridge enabled access, and the site of its abutment can still be seen. Away from the fort, near the river, lies the bath-house, one of the most evocative ruins in Roman Britain. Some of the walls stand up to 10ft high, and it is possible to sit in the changing room, in the arched cubicles which may have held clothes, or altars to Roman deities. In the *caldarium* (hot room) the bath in its corner alcove was lit by a bay window 4ft wide, the opening of which is still visible. Shattered window glass was found nearby during excavation.

The headquarters building at Chesters is the most impressive north of the Alps. Below the main standard bearer's office a sunken strongroom was discovered in 1803. The door was made of wood sheathed with iron plates rivetted together with nails. It opened inwards and was found to be in a 'sadly decayed condition'. The building still retains the third-century roof and a flagged floor.

In 1862 and 1928 an extraordinary sight was to be observed on the road near Chesters fort. Here the road metalling uses the top of the wall itself as a foundation. After a long period of wear without road repairs, the facing stones and inner core of the wall were visible in the road surface.

At the spectacular vantage point of Housesteads the remains give an extensive plan of a typical fort. The tracks worn by carts in the gateway stones bring the Romans nearer. Although the wooden seats are now missing from the latrine, the deep sewers are intact. Constant water ran through the stone gutter in front of the seats, where the soldiers could wash their sponges (the equivalent of lavatory paper). Two stone wash-basins are still in place.

From Housesteads a gentle walk leads through a coppice down to milecastle 37. The fallen voussoirs from an impressive arch lie near its northern gateway. Beyond, the wall leads to Cuddy's Crag. The steep incline has been worn slippery by countless feet (Hadrian's Wall like Snowdon is suffering from erosion by

Fig 14 Reconstruction of a gate at Housesteads fort

tourists). Further on, Crag Lough on a misty day is pencilled into the green-grey haze with deeper grey trees and hills. The water is still and timeless as a nineteenth-century watercolour. Eventually the Wall reaches a crescendo above Milking Gap, the precipitous cliffs plunging down to a milecastle in the hollow.

For such a substantial structure, it is surprising that Hadrian's Wall was not one conception. The close observer can detect many changes of policy carried out during the building operations. Excavations reveal others. The military and political expediencies of the Empire were changing rapidly in the early second century. No sooner had the legionaries put up a wall with milecastles along it, than it was decided to bring the troops forward from the Stanegate to the frontier itself. Almost as soon as a turret at Housesteads had been erected, it was demolished and replaced by the fort. Before this was finished one half of the northern gateway was blocked, presumably to minimise vulnerability to attack. Defence was suddenly the order of the day.

Milecastle 48, at Poltross Burn, drips across a slope like one of Salvador Dali's limp watches. Two stone barrack blocks are enlivened by the reddened and blackened stones of an oven. It might have been raked out only a few hours ago. In the north-east corner are slight remains of the staircase to the wall-walk. Here as at Housesteads, the gateways have been narrowed. A railway line runs alongside Poltross Burn cutting the milecastle off from the Wall with a cold wind of iron as the train rushes by.

THE ANTONINE WALL

The Antonine Wall in contrast to the more southerly boundary, has the misfortune to run through what became some of the most built-up areas in Scotland. It hides under Glasgow suburbs and pops up under electricity pylons and in the shadow of mills. Where visible, it is often no more than a low bank with a ditch (it was built of turf on a stone foundation). Where it is possible to see the foundations with their drainage channels, at New Kilpatrick Cemetery, the adjacent tombstones do nothing to evoke flights of antiquarian fancy.

In autumn, Rough Castle on the Antonine Wall, glows under a setting sun with the red-gold of bracken. The trees that in summer shadow the massive ramparts are strikingly silhouetted against the skyline. Here the fort ditches have been cleared out, and a section of the Antonine Wall ditch has been restored to more or less its original profile. Within, are the indeterminate remains of stone buildings that once housed the sixth Cohort of Nervii from the Rhine. A sinister reminder that the Roman occupation of this area was concerned with conquest lies under the vegetation near the north side of the fort. A few hollows remain of what were ten rows of *lilia* (pits in which stakes were set and camouflaged, to impale charging horsemen). At this fort is one of the best stretches of the Wall; at Watling Lodge the ditch is a formidable 40ft wide and 15ft deep, and at Croy Hill it is rock cut, though immediately east of the now vanished fort the rock was too hard for the ditch to be dug out. One of the beacon platforms used for signalling can be seen to the west of Rough Castle, and beside the Wall at this point the Military Way used for mobilising troops can be clearly seen. It can also be followed in Seabegs Wood, not far from Rough Castle.

The forts of the Antonine Wall were spaced about two miles apart, often with annexes for storing supplies and for the troops in transit to camp. Three interval fortlets are known between pairs of forts—there may have been more. Outpost forts protected the Wall. To the east and north, Fife and Strathmore were protected by forts like Ardoch at Braco. In the west the south bank of the Clyde was protected by a fort at Whitemoss and a couple of fortlets.

Just as Hadrian's Wall had its supply forts of Corbridge and South Shields, so the Antonine Wall had a supply base at Cramond on the Firth of Forth. It is here, alone of all the forts in the Antonine Wall scheme, that some consolidated foundations of fort buildings can be seen, attractively laid out in what is now a public park. The walk from the fort takes one through the picturesque village and down to the harbour, which is now as busy with holidaymakers' yachts as it must then have been with Roman supply boats. A ferry will take the seeker of Roman Britain across to the opposite shore, from which a stroll leads to a rock jutting out onto the beach. On this, behind a grill, is a worn carving. Once thought to be of an eagle (hence its name Eagle Rock) it is now believed to be of Mercury, the patron god of Roman travellers.

7 Inscriptions

The Romans had a mania for writing things down about themselves. They wrote their names on tombstones and milestones, altars, above public buildings, on tiles, metal ingots, pieces of pottery and walls. The least-important people have thus been remembered by chance, and some of the most capable or distinguished have disappeared without trace.

The art of reading inscriptions is complex despite the highly stereotyped formulae. Most inscriptions are abbreviated so that what seems to be a few letters on a tombstone can become in translation many paragraphs. The formulae are adhered to so strictly that even a small fragment of a monumental inscription can often be expanded into its much larger original. A Roman seeing S T T – on a tombstone would have been as certain that the missing letter was L, as an Englishman would be about the missing word in the phrase 'God save the – – – – –'.

This adherence to formulae means that certain categories of inscription can be recognised without a knowledge of Latin. Tombstones are recognisable from their shape—usually flat slabs with gable tops suitable for setting into walls. The inscription is set beneath the triangle of ornament at the top. STTL can often be seen at the end of the inscription and stands for the rather charming sentiment Sit Tibi Terra Levis (May the earth be light for thee). This replaced the more prosaic HSE (Hic Situs Est—He is laid here) in the second century. The beginning of tombstone inscriptions usually read DM—Dis manibus—to the souls of the departed. Anyone desecrating a monument bearing this legend would be liable to prosecution. The name of the deceased is usually put with the age, expressed very precisely to the number of days. The person erecting the tombstone is also mentioned.

Thus many of the more uneventful sides of Roman life are revealed. It is remarkable for instance that more men put up tombstones commemorating their wives in affectionate or admiring terms than women to their husbands. Whether this was because more Roman men thought themselves happy in their marriages than their wives, or because economics prevented women putting up elaborate inscriptions to their husbands, is not clear.

A sad fact of life was that although the Romans had mastered the arts of tapping water, heating their houses, even keeping liquids hot in double containers, they were unable to prevent or cure all ills. Nowhere is this harsh reality of Roman civilisation more apparent than in the inscriptions on tombstones. Few lived beyond thirty or forty, though one man in Caerleon lived to a hundred, and others lived to be sixty or seventy. Children, deeply mourned by parents, frequently died young:

> To Sucessa Petronia, who lived three years, four months and nine days; Vep—omulus and Victoria Sabina set this up to their beloved daughter

records an inscription from Bath. In 1970 a touching child's burial was found at Gatcombe, Somerset, dating from the third century. Two fragmentary boot *segs* (studs) show that it was of a boy. In the grave was a genuine late neolithic barbed and tanged arrowhead, perhaps more than two thousand years old when the burial was made, and a series of four triangular stones which looked like arrowheads. The four stones could never have been used as missiles; they, and the real arrowhead were obviously toys.

The standard of health must have been appallingly low: skirmishes or outright battles were frequent, men toiled in mines and cut down forests, the carbohydrate content of the diet caused rotting teeth and women risked lead poisoning every time they titivated themselves for a party. Medicine was primitive, though it became fashionable to invest in a medically knowledgeable slave from Greece.

Cures were mainly herbal mixtures, some of which may have been used by the druids before the coming of the Romans. Some of the herbal cures are familiar today—belladonna, cinnamon, poppy and henbane. Although cabbages and turnips are not now considered very efficacious, the latter was turned into a poultice to cure chilblains and gout. Mustard plasters (and no doubt mustard baths), and a type of dock known as *radix Britannica* seems to have been found effective as a cure for scurvy—a box lid inscribed *e radice britannica* was found in the German fort of Haltern. Eye troubles seem to have been rife, and quacks sold patent salves. The stamps that they used to mark their wares are not uncommon finds; one from Sandy, Bedfordshire, is a flat slab of stone inscribed on its faces:

Gaius Valerius Amandus' vinegar lotion for running eyes
Gaius Valerius Amandus' drops for dim sight
Gaius Valerius Valentinus' poppy ointment after an attack of inflamation of the eyes
A mixture for clearing the sight.

Not all these cures were effective, however, and by the third century tombstones became less fashionable than stone sarcophagi among the rich. Lead coffins began to be manufactured in increasing numbers, with inscriptions on them following the traditional formulae. One found at York under the booking office of the railway station preserved a lock of auburn hair pierced by jet hair pins.

More optimistic inscriptions commemorate buildings. The

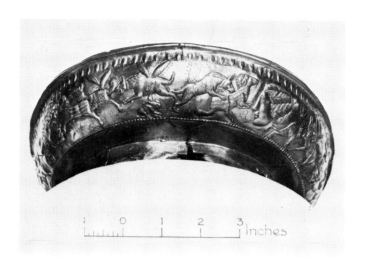

Plate 13 Part of the Traprain treasure from West Lothian. Scale $\frac{1}{2}$. *(National Museum of Antiquities of Scotland)*

Plate 14 (left) Silver bowl from the Mildenhall treasure. Scale $\frac{1}{2}$. *(British Museum)*

Plate 15 (right) The great dish from the Mildenhall silver treasure. Scale $\frac{1}{12}$. *(British Museum)*

Plate 16 (above) Portchester
Castle in Hampshire. The
south wall from the south-
west corner. (*John Bethell*)

EAST
GRANARY

Plate 17 (left) Hadrian's
Wall at Corbridge, showing
the east granary. (*Department
of the Environment*)

finest can be several feet long, beautifully inscribed and chiselled with perfect formal lettering. That from the forum at Wroxeter is exceptional, with stops in the traditional shape of vine leaves. Some were simply a check on building work, being covered over with plaster. Many such slabs can be seen along Hadrian's Wall and the Antonine Wall. Each contingent of soldiers placed a slab at the end of the stretch of wall they had just completed.

Reconstructed buildings often hide a tale of dramatic destruction. The words *vi ignis exustum*, explaining that the building was burnt down, often hides the sacking of the place by natives.

The inscriptions now to be seen in museums are simple uncoloured stones, but originally garish paint was added to emphasise the motifs or letters. A slab in Caerleon museum actually retains some fragments of paint. It commemorates work done on the amphitheatre by the century of Rufinus.

The most diverse category of inscriptions apart from graffiti are the religious dedications. Votive offerings, column bases and altars can all be found with references to various pagan gods. The distinctive shape of altars is of a shaft with base and capital. The deities are myriad—from Apollo god of the sun who drove his chariot across the sky, to Silvanus of the woods, from Minerva and Mars to Fortuna, Nemesis and Victoria. Native deities such as Ricagambeda, Nemetona or Cocidius appear more frequently than oriental gods like Serapis. Altars can often be seen bearing the formula VSLM (Votum Solvit Libens Merito—paid a vow willingly and deservedly) referring to the donor of the offering.

At Wroxeter during excavations by Thomas Wright in the late nineteenth century, part of a wall was discovered with two lines of a graffito intact. Apparently this completed an inscription found on plaster and stucco in a passage of the Baths. Unfortunately before anyone could examine it 'Two casual visitors . . . amused themselves by employing their walking sticks or umbrellas to break off the plaster in order, apparently, to try its strength'. Wright gathered up what he could, but contemporary technology did not allow any sense to be made of the pieces. The episode seems to have been fated, however, for before what remained could be drawn an 'unfortunate misunderstanding with the tenant occurred by which we were temporarily excluded from the field'. By the time the excavation resumed, the plaster was further and irretrievably damaged by the weather.

Some written evidence while saying little of factual interest can shed light on the writer. The Rudston mosaic is remarkable for having several animals set round Venus named in very bad Latin. The bull is labelled

TAV

RVS

showing that the mosaicist and possibly the original draughtsman was unfamiliar with Latin in its written form. On the whole however the Romano-Britons were remarkably literate, as graffiti show. A very human touch is revealed on a London graffito, and seems to be an observation by a potter about one of his lazy workmates 'Australis has been wandering about by himself every day for a fortnight'. A fingertip inscription by a workman at a brickworks says simply *Satis* (Enough, or 'Fed up') while a piece of high-quality samian pottery carries the simple inscription *Fur* (Thief) perhaps a warning by the servants in one house to those of the next.

Some inscriptions show an even higher standard of literacy. Tags from Virgil's *Aeneid* are not uncommon, and appear in the mosaic from Lullingstone villa, on a coin of Carausius, and even in a jumble of names and words from Silchester which seems to have been a child's writing lesson. Even more learned are the inscriptions on two bronze votive plates from York, which were dedicated by Demetrius the Scribe to the gods of the governor's praetorium, Oceanus and Tethys. The inscriptions are in Greek, and the Demetrius who dedicated them may have been none other than the Grammarian, whom Plutarch records as having visited Britain around AD 80.

A few writing tablets shed some light on little-known aspects of Roman Britain. One from Chew Stoke in Somerset is a legal text concerning the ownership of land. Of fifty or so tablets found in 1973 at Vindolanda on Hadrian's Wall, one preserves part of a letter mentioning two pairs of sandals, an unspecified number of woollen socks, and two pairs of underpants. These were probably being sent to the recipient via the bringer of the letter—Roman soldiers were responsible for their own clothing. Sandals were found with the letter, and may have been the very ones mentioned. Other tablets deal with supplies, and give an insight into the diet of Roman soldiers—wine, beer, fish-sauce, pork fat, spice, goat's milk, salt, young pig, ham, corn, venison and flour are all mentioned, as well as what they cost in some instances. Another tablet mentions the man believed to be governor of Britain in AD 103, and also the name of the place from which it was being sent, proving that the fort was known as Vindolanda as early as the beginning of the second century.

When legal means failed, the Romans had to resort to curses. In the British Museum an inscription reads 'I fix Tertia Maria and her life and mind and memory and liver and lungs mixed fate thought memory: so may she not be able to speak secrets or . . .' This particular example leaves the imagination running riot as to its ending, and the story that led to its execution. Fixing a person was a simple business which involved obtaining a suitable piece of stone or lead, inscribing it and nailing it down, often on a tomb, as a sign that the victim was given to the gods of the underworld.

8 Gods and Devils

In Castle Street, Cirencester, in the garden of Mr Isaac Tibbot, the burial of a Roman lady, Julia Casta, was discovered. The gentleman, curious as were all his eighteenth-century contemporaries, took the skull into his summerhouse, where, after a while Stukeley relates that 'People have stole all her teeth for amulets against the ague'.

The British always seem to have been superstitious about the remains of their ancestors. The manifestations of this fear are seen in such names as Grim's (ie Devil's) or Devil's Dyke, applied to earthworks of usually the most innocuous origins. Historical records seem to have been lost to the Anglo-Saxons, who occupied the old Roman areas. One writer describes the ruins, probably at Bath, as the work of Giants, all record of the real builders having been lost. Walking round Caerwent in 1976 I was struck by how easily this type of myth could have been fostered. Anglo-Saxon towns or villages required substantial defences as little as modern ones. Their houses were timber, and, compared to the walls of a Roman town or fort, flimsy, and of one storey. Without knowledge of their history, walls 8ft wide and 14ft high, enclosing up to hundreds of acres, must indeed have seemed possible only as the perimeter of the abode of a race of people of enormous capabilities.

Some superstitions were created in the period of antiquarianism. Stukeley, whose writings have featured frequently in this book, was one of the greatest eighteenth-century sufferers of 'druidomania', an affliction that led to the attribution of any structure or object of unknown origin to the ancient druids. The Roman writers, who came into contact with this priestly caste of Celts in the early days of the conquest, and who finally wrote of their capture and annihilation in Anglesey, added some hair-raising embellishments about the priests. Whether or not these stories were true is difficult to establish since such horrors as burning humans alive in giant wicker baskets obviously would leave little trace. It is not impossible that the brutality was exaggerated to emphasise the bravery and prowess of the Roman aggressors. It seems certain that the Britons under the leadership of the druids were harassing the Romans—men were given refuge on the island, and supplies were sent over to Gaul. While the druids remained an important force in politics the Roman conquest of Gaul would never be safe. The picture of a druid dancing round a rock with mistletoe garlands, is almost entirely a Romantic fantasy—they were a more down-to-earth force.

Less fanciful information about Celtic British religion can be found in many museums, especially those in northern Britain. The cult of the head, so embellished by writers on the druids, was certainly a reality. The head was regarded as the seat of the soul—good and evil alike. Headhunting took place and the gruesome trophies where exhibited above hillfort gates. A skull which had fallen from the gateway was found during the 1951–2 excavations at Stanwick, the Brigantes' capital in Yorkshire. Others were discovered where they had fallen from the gate of Bredon Hill, Gloucestershire.

Numerous stone heads were venerated. Celtic heads were totally different in conception from their classical counterparts. The sculpture is often crude and violent. Eyes stare and mouths deteriorate to a mere gash; the nose is a simple projection. It is symbolism at its most pure. The effect on modern eyes, softened by a diluted classically based culture can be terrifying, though this reaction was not the original intention. An overawing example can be seen in Tullie House Museum, Carlisle Into the $7\frac{1}{4}$in block found at Netherby, Cumberland, is packed enough force and emotion to turn back an army. The block was crudely hewn into the shape of a human head—with deep gouges for mouth and eyes. The smashed-in nose is only partly the result of accident. Broodingly it glowers at the observer. Behind the ears curl a pair of ram's horns, identifying this Celtic deity with the classical god Jupiter Amnon. A less-frightening head of about the same size was found at Corbridge and is in the site museum. The face is smoother and more Celtic, with its typical lentoid eyes and pointed chin. It is more hirsute, with a beard and drooping moustache. Its aspect is of eternal sadness rather than terror. This might have been a local god, Maponus, sometimes identified with Apollo. Its cranium was hollowed to take offerings.

Celtic religion offered a panoply of gods. Many are known from single allusions to their names, but no doubt they were local versions of certain basic deities. As time went on they became increasingly identified with Roman gods and goddesses possessing similar attributes. Thus hybrids became common. There is no mistaking whether a god is Roman or Celtic from sculpture, however, and when a hybrid occurs, the treatment of the features (symbolically if Celtic, stylistically if Roman), makes especially uneasy art.

It would be impossible to recount the numerous represent-ations in stone, in bronze or in more perishable materials that attest the devotion of the Romans to their gods; Mars, Mercury, Minerva, Juno, Apollo, Jupiter and Venus abound. They can be simple dedications thrown into springs, made perhaps from pipeclay, or elaborate and extremely accomplished art objects. There are household gods and water nymphs, mother goddesses and genii, and each deity can appear in a different guise.

RELIGIOUS ARTWORKS

One most attractive artwork was found in the Walbrook Mithraeum in London, and depicts the head of the oriental god Serapis, associated with Isis. If the head of the Celtic god from Netherby erred on the side of crudity, the studied curls of this bust err on the side of perfection. The smoothness of the cheeks, the flowing locks (two of which are broken and were meant to hang free of his face) and the upraised eyes, finely sculptured down to the details of the eyelids and carefully etched pupils, take the god away from his earthly surroundings. There is a quality of stillness and eternity in this work equalled in few other sculptures. Because the head was intended to sit in a niche, the back is flat. At some time part of the cascading hair was hewn off, perhaps in order to fit the sculpture into its niche more readily. On the head is a modius or corn measure, a symbol of fertility which distinguished Serapis from other gods.

A second outstanding example of Roman art, also found in the Walbrook Mithraeum, is a marble head of Minerva, now in the Guildhall Museum, London. The goddess' face is cold and classically dispassionate. Her mouth is perfectly sculptured, her jawline smooth, the nose and profile perfectly cut and untroubled. Across her brow is a plain band of marble, almost certainly the seating for a metal helmet, now lost. Most heads of Roman deities were originally attached to bodies made out of less durable and expensive material, which often accounts for their somewhat unfinished aspect.

BATH

Minerva is closely associated with one of the most beautiful and elegant eighteenth-century cities: Bath. Even today its spa waters are in demand, though faith in the water's curative powers is waning for the first time in two thousand years. The waters attracted the Romans (and probably the Celts before them), the Saxons, the people of the Middle Ages and especially the fashionable in the Georgian and Regency eras. Most of what is seen today is the result of the architectural skill and imagination of a Yorkshireman, John Wood, whose vision of a classical city with imperial gymnasium, forum and circus came so near to execution. While relatively little of Roman Bath remains, much of the splendour that must have delighted the many visitors lives on. Nineteenth-century Bath doubtless had much in common with the great spa town of Aquae Sulis, with the porticoed buildings, the ornate cornices, the arcades, the rows of hostelries and the bathing establishment.

The water is remarkable, still warm, though perhaps not deserving Leland's description that it 'rikith like a seething potte, continually having sumwhat a suphureus and sumwhat unpleasant flavor'. Leland made lists of ancient sites between 1536 and 1542, but before he had finished was certified insane.

By the eighteenth century the waters were treated to an even more graphic description by Stukeley:

> This water is admirably grateful to the stomach, striking the roof of the mouth with a fine sulphureus and steely gas.

It is probably not necessary to take his further advice:

> It is of a most sovereign virtue to strengthen the bowels . . . Hither let the hypochondriac student repair and drink at the Muses' spring: no doubt the advantages obtained here in abdominal obstructions must be very great.

Possibly the Romans were spurred on by similar hopes of relief when they undertook the massive construction of the city late in the first century. If a Celtic place of worship existed there, all trace would have been lost, except perhaps for the deity, Minerva-Sulis, a hybrid Roman and Celtic goddess with whom Bath was associated. The finest relief from the city which dominated a lost façade of a classical temple is the famous triangular pediment, over 26ft wide. The central head twined with wings and snakes, and with flaming hair represents Medusa who is associated with Minerva.

The structures of Roman Bath have been uncovered continuously and excavation of bath buildings necessitated shift work in hot humid conditions near the hot spring. The city is always a pleasant place to visit, and the Great Bath is still lined with its Roman lead though it is now open to the sky.

CLAUDIUS THE GOD

The Romans were not content with mythological gods. It became increasingly popular to deify the emperor, eventually while he still lived. A temple to the emperor Claudius was erected in Colchester, a fine classical building of which the concrete foundations still maintain the weight of the Norman keep. It is possible to walk below the museum (housed in the keep) under the vault-like structures, which originally were filled with sand as a constructional aid.

MITHRAISM

An extraordinary religion that came to Britain from the East was Mithraism. A number of temples dedicated to the god Mithras have been found, of which the one most notable for producing an enormous number of art objects was that on the Walbrook, London. The standing example at Carrawburgh on Hadrian's Wall is still an eerie place to visit in the early evening. Unlike most Roman buildings Mithraea were often dug out of the ground, simulating a cave. Mithras was born from a rock, and by sacrificing a large bull which he caught, won salvation for the human race. From the blood of the bull sprang the life-giving forces useful to man. Mithras is connected with

97

the sun and is often referred to as Sol Invictus, the Unconquered Sun. The evident similarity between this cult and Christianity was furthered by the ground plans of Mithraea and churches. Both are based on the Roman basilica, with two aisles each side of a nave which had an altar or altars at one end. In the Carrawburgh mithraeum a narthex allowed novices to attend worship without actually entering the nave proper.

The cult demanded very high physical and moral courage, and as such appealed to the military and men of a similar disposition (women were excluded) in commercial centres such as London. A series of tests or feats of endurance were called for before the initiate became a fully fledged member. Mithraism did not enjoy popularity with the authorities, since it demanded a devotion over and above that owed to the state. Mithraea show signs of destruction in the third century and later, especially it seems when Christianity became popular.

A relief from Housesteads dating from the second or third century shows Mithras being born not from a rock but an egg. It is framed with the signs of the zodiac, and the god sits, Buddha-like, his hands stretched out to the side, carrying a torch and a sword. The body stands out in openwork—presumably a light was set behind to illuminate the god. A similar idea can be seen on an altar from the Carrawburgh Mithraeum in which rays are cut through the thickness of the stone, to allow light to penetrate as though in a halo.

A very expressive marble relief roundel from the Walbrook Mithraeum shows Mithras slaying the bull. A dog and a snake jump up to lick its blood, while a scorpion attacks it. On either side are Mithras' assistants Cautes, bearing an upright torch (symbol of light) and Cautopates, bearing an inverted one (symbol of darkness and turmoil). In Newcastle Museum of Antiquities there is a reconstruction (actual size) of the interior of the Mithraeum, garishly coloured, quite different from the grey remains at Carrawburgh.

CHRISTIANITY

Few relics of Christianity remain in Britain—a few mosaics, the occasional inscription and some objects which could, but need not have, a Christian significance. A famous cryptogram was found in the nineteenth century on a piece of wall plaster in Cirencester, reading

ROTAS

OPERA

TENET

AREPO

SATOR

This translates as 'Arepo the sower guides the wheels with work' and apart from reading the same both down and across, the letters can be re-arranged to give Pater Noster, A and O (the first words of the Lord's Prayer between alpha and omega). The Cirencester inscription probably dates from the second century, but as the same formula appears in Herculaneum in the first century at a date that seems too early for Christianity, it may have been a popular puzzle taken up by Christians, and is not in itself positive proof of the belief.

Christianity undoubtedly became popular in Britain, especially in the fourth century. The most dramatic incident was the martyrdom of St Alban, which took place in Verulamium (hence the modern name St Albans) probably at the very end of the second century. By the fourth century Britain had Bishops (who boasted they were too poor to go to the Council of Arles), and in AD 429 St Germanus arrived to stamp out a British heresy, Pelagianism, proving that Christianity was so well established that heresy was a problem.

In 1975 one of the most exciting treasures to be found came to light in the fields near Water Newton. Silverwork and a piece of gold made up the hoard, which seems to have been of church plate of the third century AD. The hoard included a chalice, plate (possibly a paten?) and various votive plaques, some with Chi-Rho symbols on them. News of this find came to me along a tortuous grapevine before it was made public. It had turned up by chance during the fieldwalking of an amateur archaeologist, and naturally, to avoid damage by treasure hunters, the exact findspot was suppressed. Rumours abounded, but I could find out nothing about the actual location of the discovery until a friend telephoned me from East Anglia to say that the discovery was common knowledge locally. Even in these days of sophisticated communication, news travels slowly by word of mouth. Like many treasures, this one was not recognised when it came out of the ground; the finder assumed it was pewter, and left it in a garden shed.

Lullingstone, already described as the development of a secular site, is unique for its religious associations. The story of the villa exemplifies the changing religious views of the Britons during the Roman period. From British farmer to sophisticated pagan Roman to Romano-British Christian, the villa saw four centuries of change. It is unique among religious remains; the beauty of the mosaics depicting classical myths, the exquisite workmanship of the portrait busts that became revered, the lovely wall paintings of water nymphs, are surpassed nowhere in the British Isles. And the conflict between Christian and pagan beliefs is especially poignant at Lullingstone where the portraits of the former owners were accorded a reverence by their new owners who were unable, despite their differing beliefs, to relegate their shades to obscurity and degradation.

The story begins almost at the start of the life of the villa. In the late first century, when the farmer owner had just started to acquire Roman tastes, a small temple to a Roman or Romano-British deity was built on a terrace behind the house. It was an unimposing circular thatched hut, apparently without a window, since no glass was found nearby. The tessellated floor was red and yellow, set off with red and white painted walls. An altar or cult object stood at one side. It was only one step more romanised than the traditional British grove.

When the villa changed hands, the owner added a new set of cult rooms to cater for his more classical taste. The Deep Room was now decorated lavishly and fitted out for the veneration of the water nymphs. A thick concrete floor was laid and tiled steps led up to the house. A square pit, 3ft deep, was sunk

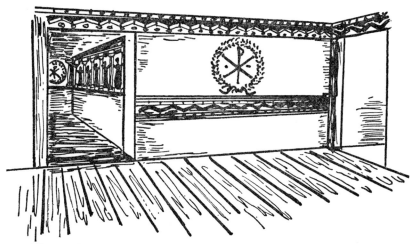

Fig 15 Reconstruction of the Christian rooms, Lullingstone villa

into the floor for a spring, opposite a niche painted with three nymphs. The paintings were of fine Mediterranean execution— one nymph stood in the centre with a seated companion at each side. Green leaves were twined in their hair, blue necklaces encircled their necks, and water cascaded from the central figure's breasts.

The wall near the stairway was painted to represent a balustrade in red and yellow trellis. The colours were light and happy, enchanting relics of a belief that was abandoned only through the disaster that struck at the end of the century (p 42).

When the new owners took over the villa after a period of dereliction, they discovered the marble portrait busts somewhere in the house where they had been abandoned by the previous family. Reverently they placed them on the steps of the Deep Room shrine. The water nymph paintings were covered with a hurried lick of red and white paint, and two votive pots were placed in the concrete floor. One was a common cooking pot, the other a pretty painted Rhenish jar inscribed in white with the word SVAVIS (sweet). Inside was the rib of a sheep— perhaps the remains of a feast given by the new owners to satisfy the souls of the old represented by the portrait marbles.

Pagan beliefs were kept alive in the mosaics (pp 42–3 and in the temple-mausoleum which was built around AD 300 behind the house. Over a square tomb for a young man and woman in their early twenties was a painted chamber for the rituals associated with keeping their memory alive. The two decorated lead coffins were placed in a wooden sarcophagus with grave goods suitable for the after-life—two spoons and knives, two glass bowls and flagons and four glass bottles. The burial was then covered with twelve layers of gravel and chalk—the weight of which eventually caused the sarcophagus to collapse. When this happened the temple was in ruins and the coffin of the young woman was removed and robbed. Her bones were thrown carelessly back into the grave.

The demise of interest in the mausoleum and its associated pagan rituals came with the conversion of the family to Christianity some time in the late fourth century. The relics of this belief are unique at Lullingstone. Eventually the granary went out of use and it can be inferred that the sole use of the house was for Christian purposes.

Redecoration transformed the rooms above the pagan shrine unmistakably into a Christian chapel. A brightly-coloured fresco of figures in the characteristic praying position (arms outstretched) dominated the room. With blue and saffron robes, edged with pearls the orantes stand with a curtain behind them, perhaps indicating that they were already thought of as dead.

Even more conclusively Christian were the fragments of plaster that, painstakingly pieced together like a jig-saw, formed a Chi-Rho monogram. Brilliant red on a white background, with a surrounding wreath of polychrome flowers and leaves, it impressed itself on anyone entering the suite of rooms.

With the religious schizophrenia of the times, someone, whilst the Christian rooms were in use above, spread a new clay floor over the still pagan Deep Room. Two fresh pottery offerings were set in the floor. Thus the two beliefs continued side by side until a fire brought destruction in the fifth century.

In the late-Roman period, when the political hold of Rome was becoming more tenuous, there was an upsurge of pagan Celtic beliefs; with a difference. The little temple at Lydney exemplifies this. High in the woods above the valley of the Severn, in the late fourth century, a temple and hostelries for guests were established. The god venerated was Nodens, not a common deity, but apparently connected with water and with healing. It has been suggested that he is Nuadd Lud, the very common Irish god with whom Bath is connected in medieval stories. Could it be that here, as elsewhere, the natives finding the old Roman gods as useless politically as the Celtic ones had been during the conquest were adopting the gods of the incoming raiders and settlers from Ireland? We perhaps shall never know. But what is certain is that in the last days of Roman Britain old beliefs stirred in the blood of the Romano-Britons. Nowhere can this be more clearly seen than at Maiden Castle, where within the ramparts of the fort which had once been held by the Durotriges and had fallen to Vespasian, a little shrine was built in the fourth century. The wheel had come the full circle, the natives were coming into their own.

9 History through Coins

One of the rarest coins in the British Isles is a silver piece with CARA on the obverse next to the head of Hercules in a lion's skin. On the reverse there is an eagle standing on a serpent. This coin was struck by one of the earliest heroes in British history, Caratacus, prince of the Catuvellauni.

In 40 or 41, on the eve of the conquest, the great king Cunobelin died, and the stability of British politics was shattered. His two sons, Caratacus and Togodumnus, began a programme of expansion and probably overran the Dobunni. Verica of the Atrebates was expelled and forced to flee. Rome, after Caesar's campaigns in Britain, was the ally of the Atrebates, and now had the excuse for conquest. The lure of riches, the desire of Claudius to make an important conquest, the presence of the disturbing druidical power, added to the reasons behind the invasion. Caratacus finally fled to South Wales where he incited the Silures to an aggressive policy. In 47 he moved to the territory of the Ordovices in Snowdonia. A massed battle ended in his family being captured and Caratacus escaping by horse to the Brigantes. Alas, he had misjudged the politics once more: he was handed captive to his enemies and apparently processed in chains through the streets of Rome. 'Nothing appaled by this adversity' he delivered this speech, here quoted from Tacitus by William Camden the sixteenth-century antiquary and historian:

> Had my moderation and carriage in prosperity been answerable
> to my nobility and estate, I might have come hither rather a

friend than a captive . . . my present state as it is reproachful to me, so is it honourable to you: I had horsemen, munition and money; what marvel is it if I were loth to lose them? If you will be sovereign over all, by consequence all must serve you; had I yielded at the first, neither my power nor your glory had been renouned, and after my execution oblivion had ensued; but if you save my life I shall for ever be a president and proof of your clemency.

(*Remains Concerning Britain*)

This 'manly speech' of dubious logic, so appealed to the Roman admiration of oratory that his pardon was apparently purchased, though his final fate is unknown.

Coins, so frequently made from the most attractive metals, have both the allure of buried treasure, and, paradoxically, the disappointments of ugly objects. While some are perfect works of art, others are mere lumps of depressing metal with mere apologies for legends and types. Yet they bring to life the personalities and defeats, the victories and bids for power of many people whose lives directly influenced the history of Britannia.

A member of Cunobelin's family, possibly that great king himself, had a coin of Augustus made into a pendant which was found in the Lexden tumulus, near Colchester. Only men who respected the name of the founder of the Empire could have owned such an object. The Britons, even those who fought hard for independence, recognised the mystique of Rome long before the conquest. The making of coins was itself a civilised trait.

The Atrebates and the Catuvellauni had with other tribes emulated the Romans by minting their own coins before the conquest. They are extraordinary objects—some as fine as authentic classical currency, but others copies of copies of copies. Where the original showed a horse, the Celtic coin might bear nothing but dismembered limbs. A head, originally with finely drawn curls, can degenerate into an astonishing jumble of circles. However shoddy the workmanship, the pre-conquest coins prove the reverence with which the Britons regarded the Empire.

COMMEMORATIVE COINS

Roman coins were the medium of propaganda—each letter, each element in the picture had a role to play.

An aureus minted in Rome in AD 49–50 depicts the bust of a man, surrounded by lettering, and on the reverse a stylised archway surmounted by a horseman and two figures. The letters DE BRITANN are written across the arch. The lettering (the legend

Fig 16   Coins of Claudius and Antoninus Pius commemorating British victories

reads TI CLAVD CAESAR AVG P M TR P VIII IMP XVI) follows the formulae used on inscriptions of a more monumental nature; it proclaims that the bust is of Tiberius Claudius, Caesar Augustus, Pontifex Maximus (Chief Priest), Holder of the Tribunician power for eight years, hailed emperor for sixteen years. The arch on the reverse of this Claudian aureus refers to a triumphal archway erected in Rome in AD 44. The figures that surmount it are of the victorious emperor between two trophies and the inscription confirms that it was set up to commemorate the emperor's British victories. Anyone handling a coin with this type anywhere in the Empire would have been in no doubt that Claudius had been the instigating force behind the conquest of Britannia. Other coins with slightly different types can be seen to commemorate the same event.

The emperor on this De Britann coin is laureate, a finely executed portrait, carefully studied in order to bring out his character while slightly glorifying it. Roman coin engravers were masters of the art of accurate portraiture, which nevertheless succeeded in making the emperor look slightly more than a man. Their skills were sorely tried on the features of the flabby and effete Nero, but their art triumphed and the emperor appears on coins as a visionary, his uptilted chin gazing heavenwards with the wisdom of the divinely inspired Alexander. (How better to obscure his multiple chins?)

In 1958 at Bredgar in Kent thirty-four gold coins were found in a hoard, the latest of which were four of Claudius struck in AD 41–2. It is thought to be the savings of a soldier in the invading army. Having buried his money for safety before the first major battle with the Britons he may not have lived to recover it.

Coins of Hadrian are directly concerned with Britain, a reflection of that able emperor's interest in her defences. One coin, minted in Rome, shows the personification of Britannia seated with one foot on a pile of stones; almost certainly a representation of Hadrian's Wall. The figure of Britannia was modelled on other seated personifications found originally on Greek coins. It was to have a new lease of life in the reign of Charles II, who copied the type of Hadrian (giving it certain features of the Duchess of Richmond). Once re-introduced it remained in use until decimalisation.

Despite the short life of the Antonine Wall, success in the north was obviously gained, since a series of coins were minted to denote victory. Significantly too, when Britannia appears on the coins of Antoninus Pius (AD 138–61) she is in an attitude of dejection. Many of the 'Britannia' issues of this emperor are crude, and many may have been struck in the province, possibly on Hadrian's Wall.

The largest collection of Britannia coins were found in a well dedicated to Coventina, a water nymph. 327 coins of this type were found in the deposit of between 15,000 and 20,000 at Carrawburgh on Hadrian's Wall.

THIRD-CENTURY INFLATION

Early in the third century a new coin was introduced, the double denarius or antoninianus, named after the emperor Caracalla (whose name was Antoninus). The new coin, introduced as a result of inflation, was soon reduced in size until it was little bigger than the old denarius, and contained progressively less silver.

A huge hoard of antoniniani of the early third century was found in 1936 at Dorchester, Dorset. It consisted of 22,000 base silver coins, ranging in date from about AD 200 to 260, buried in a bowl, a jug and a metal box. The majority of the coins were of Philip I and Gordian III, and the hoard may have been the imperial tax collection for the city.

The confused politics of the third century affected economics. Copies of coins were struck in Britain, which often have blundered legends—at worst, mere jumbles of letters. Known as 'barbarous radiates' because they imitate coins that show the emperor wearing a radiate crown, they often have a certain naïve attraction. The economic problems of the century are not without interest today—inflation was rife, and a series of debasements and devaluations eventually brought the Empire to its knees. Debasement led to a loss of faith in official coinage with the result that older, better coins were hoarded and good money was in short supply. It was this dearth of small change that led to the proliferation of forgers' workshops. So copious are the barbarous radiates that one must infer that many were struck by semi-official mints in towns.

CARAUSIUS

Among all this third-rate coinage, it is therefore both surprising and welcome to find that the coins of the usurper Carausius and his murderer Allectus are outstanding. Gold, silver and copper coins were minted by the Menapian in Rouen, London, Colchester and possibly, but by no means certainly, Richborough. On some the legend AVGGG can be seen. This is not a misprint for AVG (claiming the Augustus title, and thus to be emperor), but a more subtle and ambitious declaration. It is a reference to Carausius and the two official emperors (Augusti), Diocletian and Maximianus.

From this time onwards the Empire was divided for ease of administration into East and West. Carausius, not content with a subtle claim to the throne, made his intention absolutely clear on other coins which read CARAVSIVS ET FRATRES SVI (Carausius and his Brothers). The obverse depicts the jugate heads of Carausius and the emperors Diocletian and Maximianus, each wearing a cuirass and sometimes with their hands upraised in greeting. The reverse carries a personification of Peace, holding an olive branch, and the proud legend PAX AVGGG.

As befitted a regime that produced such lovely monetary works of art, the final defeat of Allectus by Constantius Chlorus in AD 296 was celebrated by the minting of a unique medallion in Trier. This is an outstanding and unique piece. Struck in gold, it was found in a hoard of medallions and jewellery at Beaurains near Arras in September 1922. On the reverse the conqueror, Constantius, is seen approaching the city gates on horseback and is being welcomed by the kneeling figure of the city goddess. The abbreviation LON beneath her leaves no doubt that she was Londinium. Constantius is styled 'Restorer of the Eternal Light', the blessings of Roman civilisation having been withheld from Britain for nine years.

FOURTH-CENTURY ECONOMIC PROBLEMS

The economic problems were not at an end, however, and the fourth century, paradoxically the heyday of luxurious living, started off with measures to counteract inflation. Diocletian tried to put matters right by striking good coinage of silver which was to retain its stability in relation to gold. Unfortunately the emperor continued to strike silver-washed bronze coins and the system collapsed. It became almost impossible to regulate the coinage, and eventually the government resorted to extracting taxes in the form of clothing, food or metal bullion.

In 301 Diocletian published what was in effect a price freeze —an edict of maximum prices. Prices had soared, but the freeze merely caused hardship. The edict also tried to control employment by making it difficult for people who wished to follow careers other than those of their fathers.

All the coinage troubles of this period are reflected in Britain. Most Roman sites produce enormous numbers of fourth-century coins struck in bronze (though almost no silver or gold), for when people dropped them there seemed little point in picking them up, so little were they worth.

In spite of general inflation the fourth century was a period of remarkable prosperity for Roman Britain, already seen in mosaics and civilian life. A mint was opened in London (or possibly taken over from Allectus) in the time of Constantius Chlorus, and remained in operation until around AD 326. Later in the fourth century there was another wave of imitations of official coins in Roman Britain—ironically the coins copied were issues with the reverse legend FEL TEMP REPARATIO ('The Renewal of Happy Times').

At the end of the fourth century, after the barbarians had overrun the Wall in 367, there emerged out of the campaigns, Magnus Clemens Maximus (Maxen Wledig) (p 9). He appears not merely in medieval fantasy but on coins. When this usurper had crossed the Channel in his bid for power, he struck coins at a mint in Trier. A few bear the mint signature AVG, which might refer to London, which was renamed Augusta in the fourth century. One coin of the AVG mint depicts two emperors facing one another seated, holding a globe. The legend VICTORIA AVGG has been taken to indicate that Maximus claimed to be a colleague of the eastern emperor Theodosius. Like Carausius' before him this arrogant claim came to no good, for, invading Italy, Magnus Maximus was captured and executed by the very emperor he claimed as his colleague.

Magnus was not the last of the usurpers. Rome sent in the Vandal commander Stilicho who defeated the Picts and Scots in a campaign commemorated in a poem of Claudian in 399. But within three years he withdrew his troops to the more troubled borders on the continent, to fight the Goths. The Britons, left now with almost no troops, with a border area unmanned, raised further usurpers to the purple, Marcus in 406 and Constantine III in c 407.

For some extraordinary reason, possibly to gain official recognition, instead of looking to the defences of Britain the latter emperor crossed to the continent to secure the Rhine frontier. The Britons in 410 expelled his governors, rebelled against him and asserted too late their loyalty to Honorius. The true emperor was beset with difficulties in other parts of the Empire, and not surprisingly answered the appeal for help with a message that the British should organise their own defence. The province of Britannia was effectively lost.

The coinage of Rome was not forgotten, however. Coins were no longer minted, and the society that eventually became dominant required no such commercial niceties. Just as the pre-Roman British princes had revered the name of Augustus and the Empire, the Anglo-Saxons appear to have retained some of this mystique. Many Anglo-Saxon graves have been found to contain old Roman coins. Their owners could not have used them commercially, and probably came upon them as chance finds. But the myth of Rome was enough to give these pathetic discs of metal a significance far in excess of anything the Saxons could produce themselves. In the fullness of time, when the Anglo-Saxons came to strike coins, they often copied old Roman designs, including the 'wolf and twins' type which adorned the reverse of the small bronze coins struck by Constantine I in honour of Rome. Coins produced before and after the Roman period epitomised the greatness of the Roman civilisation possibly even more than coins produced during it.

Epilogue—Independence

In a dimly lit glass-case in the National Museum of Antiquities, Edinburgh, on the most northerly border of the Empire, glint the silver of chalices, spoons, bowls, hacksilver and coins found in 1919 at Traprain Law, East Lothian.

A flagon from the hoard, almost whole, is decorated with two friezes of Christian significance, one showing biblical scenes— the Fall, the Betrayal, the Adoration of the Magi, and Moses bringing water from the rock. The treasure is fine Roman table-ware, the kind that adorned many rich dining-rooms in late Roman Britain and Gaul and it is a fitting place to end this search for Roman Britain. The Votadini who lived in Traprain had enjoyed good relations with Rome. Subsequent generations of rulers traced their king-lists back to men with mysterious names—Uetern and Potern Pesrut. Behind these Celticisations, like that of Maxen Wledig, lie Roman names—Aeternus and Paternus. It has been suggested that the tribe had been supervised in the late Roman period by a decurion. But the treasure at Traprain does not seem to be the rewards of allegiance, as enjoyed by the Atrebates in the south. It is hacked up, and contains pieces that undoubtedly came from Germany—almost certainly this was loot. Despite the pro-Roman policy of the tribe, by the time the Wall had been overrun by their neighbours, the Votadini were willing to plunder civilisation. There was no doubt that without the force of the army, Roman civilisation could not exist, despite the obvious reverence with which it was regarded.

Independence had been fought for by Caratacus, Albinus Carausius and Maximus, albeit for reasons of personal ambition. Their bids had failed and when the Britons finally found themselves alone, they were disoriented and disorganised. The northern frontier had been almost a myth for decades. Wales had been settled by the Irish in the second century. Germanic tribesmen not only raided and settled in Britain but had also been drafted into the army. The threat from barbarians at the end of the era must have been more against a way of life than life itself. There is no evidence of the widespread massacres described by early historians, nor of terrified Britons fleeing westwards from Saxon threats. Indeed much evidence points to the opposite. Pottery with Roman and Saxon characteristics is common even before the fifth century—and where the ceramics had mingled, so too, surely must their users. Significantly, where early Anglo-Saxon settlements have been found they show no strong defences, as would be expected of people making a precarious living under constant threat from the Britons.

As the Britons had approached the Roman invaders, so they faced up to the new era. Some were friendly and intermingled easily, others fought on. Their efforts were fated. Perhaps the last of the freedom fighters was Arthur. Paradoxically his cause was directly descended from that of Caractacus who fought the Britons against Rome. Arthur fought for Britain too—but a Britain that had become Roman. The myths and fables that surrounded the king have been obscure until recently. The hill-fort at South Cadbury has been claimed to be the citadel from which Arthur launched his campaigns against the Saxons, culminating in his victory at the Battle of Badon in AD 495. If he did not live there, then it must have been in similar circumstances. At Cadbury the Iron Age fort was refurbished when the legions had left. It was given a Roman-style gateway and palisade, and no doubt the inhabitants attempted to keep alive the language and manners of Rome. Even the excavations have not discovered what happened eventually to this, most famous of British heroes. Like most good heroes, however, his memory lived on.

When the Normans arrived, Arthur was called on to return once more. By now the Anglo-Saxons, his traditional enemies, had become so civilised and identified themselves so closely with the island that their conquerors hoping to gain respectability, adopted him for their own.

Later, under the Tudors, the name of Arthur was once more resurrected. The new kings, wishing to add respectability to their dynasty found in Arthur a suitable hero. It was merely a cruel blow of fate that prevented Henry VIII's brother Arthur from becoming king. The legendary Arthur was given medieval clothes and speeches, a medieval hall and all the necessary pageantry. Minstrels sang his praises from Scotland to Cornwall and each locality claimed him as their own ancestor. The ghost of Arthur was called on to return in the hour of the Britons' need. Under the embellishments, stripped down to the original, the ghost of Arthur is none other than the ghost of Britannia returning with every sherd of Roman pottery dug out of a country garden, and with every scratched initial on the walls of ancient churches like Escomb.

Appendix I:

How to Find Roman Britain

The traveller in Roman Britain should begin by equipping himself with good maps and guides. As most guides give National Grid references for sites, a road atlas which utilises the National Grid is obviously useful —the *AA Great Britain Road Atlas* is particularly good. For those intending to concentrate on a particular area, the Ordnance Survey One-Inch maps relevant to the area are an advantage. A few maps mark Roman sites. The Ordnance Survey *Map of Ancient Britain* (North and South Sheets) is the most useful, as it shows ancient sites as an overprint on a modern map. The Ordnance Survey *Map of Roman Britain* is confusing for the traveller, as it does not show modern roads and marks sites where nothing is visible above ground, though it is indispensable for finding areas of Roman occupation. The Ordnance Survey maps of *Hadrian's Wall* and *The Antonine Wall* are ideal for exploring these areas.

No traveller in Roman Britain should be without R. J. A. Wilson's *Guide to the Roman Remains in Britain* (Constable, 1975), which lists everything there is to see and gives instructions on how to find it. A few other traveller's guides are useful, especially if you are interested in seeing remains of other periods as well. Of these, the best is J. Hawkes' *Guide to the Prehistoric and Roman Monuments in England and Wales* (Revised Edition 1973, Cardinal paperbacks). Also useful is H. Priestley's *Observer's Book of Ancient and Roman Britain* (1976), and for particular areas the Heinemann and Shire regional archaeologies.

PLANNING YOUR VISITS

If you have never visited any Roman sites, it is probably best not to begin by visiting minor sites where the remains are slight, but to concentrate instead on the sites which are laid out for the public. A list of these is given on p 122. Many have site museums and guidebooks which will help you understand them, and very often there are labels on individual buildings or features of interest saying what they are. Don't just wander round aimlessly thinking 'Isn't it wonderful that all this has survived nearly two thousand years' but be on the look-out for specific things and have certain questions in mind. If you are visiting a Roman fort, have in your mind the plan of a typical Roman fort, and make a point of looking for the headquarters building and commandant's house, the granaries, the barrack blocks, the gateways and the fort ditch. Explore outside the fort, if this is possible, to see if there are any buildings which lie beyond it, or a parade ground or amphitheatre. If you have a guidebook it will tell you, but it is often interesting to look in any case as guidebooks have a habit of mentioning only features which are clearly visible. If you are visiting a villa, look out for mosaics and the bathing facilities—look for the hypocausts of the central heating (these of course can be seen in town and fort buildings too), and work out which rooms were dining-rooms, public rooms, and so on. In towns, try to work out the original size of the town—again guidebooks and plans will help—and if possible try to walk from one side to the other to get an impression of its scale. Always ask yourself of any structure 'Is this typical?' and if it isn't, ask yourself what the reasons might have been for planning it differently from the usual.

I find it useful to go round a site twice, once to get my bearings and find out where particular buildings are in relation to one another, what the setting is like and whether there is any outlying feature of note. Then I study the plan of the site if there is one, and read the guide to see if there are features particularly to be noticed, before going round it again. If there is a site museum, go round it before going round the site, as it will often give you the essential information you need to make the guidebook that much more intelligible—guidebooks usually have far too much information to be understood on the site, and often unfortunately have fold-out plans which blow out in the wind and tear.

Once you have got the 'feel' of Roman sites, you can start on the refinements of site visiting. Learn to recognise Roman masonry, which is often quite distinctive. Look out for the tile courses—lines of bright orange-red tiles characteristic of Roman work. Recognise too Roman ashlar (dressed masonry). The Romans used small, neatly dressed and even stones for the facing of their walls, laid regularly like bricks—the corners can have more massive quoins (corner stones). This neatness often enables you to tell Roman from medieval masonry, and it is worth looking at walls which have Roman lower courses and medieval upper ones, which shows the contrast. The multi-angular tower in York is a good example of this, and sections of the town wall at Chester also show this feature. Don't however expect all Roman masonry to be neat—often the facing stones have been stolen or have fallen, leaving just the rubble core, bonded with cement. Roman cement is also distinctive, and experience will tell you how to recognise it. Look out too for putlog holes in the walls—round holes which once took timbers. When you can recognise Romany masonry, you can then begin to recognise later additions or reconstructions. In the fort at Hardknott, for example, the walls have been rebuilt in the Roman fashion with Roman stones for the top few courses—here the later work is recognisable because it is set back slightly from the line of the Roman original.

It is worth trying to distinguish between the different phases of building where a site has been occupied for a long time. A sure sign of a later addition is a butt-jointed wall, that is, a wall built up against another but not bonded with it, so that there is a straight joint. This can be seen for example at Caerwent, where the bastions on the town wall are butt-jointed to it, showing that they are later additions. At Caerwent too can be seen another feature worth looking out for—a blocked doorway. This is visible in the south gateway of the fort. Blocked doorways are recognisable because of the butt-jointing of the blocking, and also because they often have different masonry from the surrounding stonework. Gateways are also sometimes narrowed by the addition of some stonework—this can be seen for example at milecastle 37 on Hadrian's Wall. Rooms can sometimes be divided up with partition walls. This can clearly be seen at Fishbourne, where a mosaic was ruined by having a wall built across it.

VISITING MUSEUMS

A list of museums with interesting collections of Romano-British objects are given on p 129. As with sites, it is pointless wandering aimlessly round a museum looking at everything. Find out what are the most important objects in the museum's Romano-British collection, and begin by looking at those. If the museum is noted for its collection from a particular site, look at that next. Most of the Romano-British exhibits in museums are pots or parts of pots, bits of building materials such as tiles, and collections of coins and brooches. Usually, once you know what these types of object look like, they can be ignored as they are much the same throughout Roman Britain, and instead you should look at the more unusual small objects that help to bring the Romans to life. A very useful book which shows you what you can expect in museums is the British Museum *Guide to the Antiquities of Roman Britain*.

TAKING IT FURTHER

Once your appetite has been whetted for Romano-British archaeology you may wish to take it further. There are a number of ways you can do this. You can begin by reading some books on the subject, the best to begin with being Joan Liversidge's *Britain in the Roman Empire* (1968; Cardinal paperback edition, 1973). The standard history is S. S. Frere's *Britannia* (2nd edition, 1974, Cardinal paperbacks), and a useful if slightly out-of-date introduction is provided by I. A. Richmond's *Roman Britain*, in the Penguin History of England (1963). A simpler account of Romano-British life is provided by A. Birley's *Life in Roman Britain* (Batsford, 1964). The standard account of the archaeology, strictly for afficionados, is R. G. Collingwood and I. A. Richmond's *Archaeology of Roman Britain* (Methuen, 1969). All these books have good bibliographies. A few other lavishly illustrated books are worth reading:

Cunliffe, B.	*Fisbourne, a Roman Palace and its Garden* (Thames & Hudson, 1971)
Cunliffe, B.	*Roman Bath Discovered* (Routledge, 1971)
Meates, G. W.	*Lullingstone Roman Villa* (Heinemann, 1955)
Toynbee, J. M. C.	*Art in Roman Britain* (Phaidon, 1963)
Wacher, J.	*The Towns of Roman Britain* (Batsford, 1975)

A good way of learning more about Roman Britain in to attend adult education classes on the subject. These are usually organised by University Extra-Mural Departments, and courses offered vary from place to place and year to year. To find out if there are any in your area, write to the Extra-Mural Department of the University which serves your area. The WEA also organise such courses, and information can be obtained from the local office. If you don't know where to ask, your local library will be able to tell you, and may have details of other courses, as may your local museum.

There are many local archaeological societies which offer lectures, visits to sites and excavations and which publish journals and other booklets on aspects of local archaeology including Romano-British. A list of these is published in the *Archaeologist's Yearbook* which is an annual publication (Dolphin Press), but you can also find out about your local society from your museum or possibly your library. Your local museum will probably organise various events for the archaeologically-minded, some of which may involve Roman Britain; enquire.

There is an annual journal dealing with Romano-British archaeology —*Britannia*—published by the Society for the Promotion of Roman Studies. It is, however, pretty technical, though it provides a list of all the Romano-British discoveries in the past year.

If you would like to join a dig as a volunteer, again your local museum or local society may be able to help. A list of excavations which require volunteers is published monthly from March to September by the Council of British Archaeology, 7 Marylebone Road, London NW1. It is called the *Calendar of Excavations*. The Council for British Archaeology will be able to tell you about other local archaeological activities.

EXTENDING THE FRONTIERS

As you acquire more information, you will find that you are able to contribute to the advancement of knowledge about Roman Britain. One of the exciting things about archaeology is the fact that it is not just something that is reserved for the experts—the amateur has an important role to play, and were it not for him far less would be known about the past. Obviously, if you take part in excavations as a volunteer, you are aiding the advancement of knowledge, but you can make an even more useful contribution by observing and recording Roman remains. Many Roman sites are discovered each year by amateurs combing their own areas for the traces of earthworks or for telltale potsherds or Roman tiles lying on the surface of fields which indicate the presence of a Roman site. There is always that bit more to find in Roman Britain.

Places to Visit in Roman Britain

The following list has been classified to help you find the kind of sites that are most likely to appeal to you. The first list is of the best sites in Roman Britain from the point of view of the tourist; sites where there is a lot to see and information available. In many cases shelter is available, and many of the sites have other amenities. Those marked * are State owned. The second list is of town sites, where the Roman remains are scattered throughout the town and cannot be found without the aid of a guidebook or information from the local museum. The third list is of other places with visible remains of Roman Britain, which may be very fragmentary.

Sites in the country often have the added advantage of being in attractive scenery, are usually more evocative than town sites, and are often in remote situations; it may not be possible to get right up to them by car, and there may be no public transport. They are, however, often difficult to find without large-scale maps and are usually remote from amenities like cafes and shops. Where the sites are not State owned, they are usually on private land, and permission must be sought from the landowner before you investigate them.

Town sites are often in the most beautiful of Britain's towns, and there are often medieval and later remains as well as those of the Roman period to attract the visitor. They are usually easy of access by car or public transport, and have amenities nearby. Their main disadvantages lie in the fact that the remains are usually very fragmentary and difficult to find, and they are seldom suitable for picnics! It is also difficult to imagine the sites as they would have been in Roman times because of their built-up surroundings.

S = Admission times standard (March–April 9.30–5.30, Sundays 2–5.30; May–September 9.30–7, Sundays 2–7; October 9.30–5.30, Sundays 2–5.30; November–February 9.30–4, Sundays 2–4).
A = Open at any reasonable time.
Sm = Sunday mornings from 9.30 April–September.
* = State owned.

The reference given in brackets after the site name is the National Grid Reference.

THE BEST SITES IN ROMAN BRITAIN

*Richborough, Kent (TR 3260) **S Sm** 1½m NW of Sandwich, off the A257. Very extensive remains of successive forts. Small site museum. Masonry up to 20ft high. *Rutupiae*. (See p 72)

*Pevensey, Kent (TQ 6404) **A** Between Eastbourne and Hastings on A259. Impressive remains of fort—all but top additions to walls are Roman. *Anderida*.

*Lullingstone, Kent (TQ 5365) **S Sm** Signposted road off A225 at Eynsford. Good remains of villa and mosaics. (See p 40, 100)

*Portchester, Hants (SU 6204) **A** Signposted on A27 between Farnham and Portsmouth. Extremely impressive and well-preserved fort. Walls over 20ft high, fourteen original bastions. Medieval additions including castle.

*Burgh Castle, Suffolk (TG 4704) **A** 2m SW of Great Yarmouth, off A143. Fort with masonry 15ft high and 8ft thick. *Garrianorum*. (See p 72)

*Wroxeter, Salop (SJ 5608) **S** off B4380, 5m SE of Shrewsbury. Town with extensive remains, baths, Forum portico base, and massive masonry of gymnasium wall ('The Old Work') standing. *Viroconium Cornoviorum*. (See p 46)

*Wall, Staffs (SK 0906) **S** 2m SW of Lichfield, off A5. Fairly impressive bath-house and other remains, being excavated. Town. *Letocetum*.

*Caerleon, Gwent (ST 3490) 3m NE of Newport, 1½m from intersection 25 on M4. Fortress of Second Legion. Multiple banks of fortress with barracks and ovens (Admission times: **A**). Very impressive amphitheatre, dug by Sir Mortimer Wheeler and associated in legend with King Arthur (Admission times: **S**). *Isca*. (See p 66)

*Brecon Gaer, Powys (SO 0029) **A** 2m W of Brecon, off the A40. Fort with three gateways, angle turret and part of wall.

*Caernarvon, Gwynedd (SH 4862) **S** On outskirts of town, on A4085 to Beddgelert. Fort with wall, gates and many internal buildings. *Segontium*.

*Caerwent, Gwent (ST 4690) **A** On the A48, about 5m W of Chepstow. Fine circuit of town walls, furnished with bastions, within which is modern village. Roman foundations of shops and temple within village. *Venta Silurum*. (See p 55)

*Hardknott, Cumbria (NY 2101) **A** Side road off A593, about 10m W of Ambleside. Outstandingly positioned fort commanding pass. Well preserved walls, gates and some internal buildings. Site of parade ground. (See p 63)

Hadrian's Wall

*Corbridge, Northumberland (NY 9864) **S Sm** ½m W of modern Corbridge. Supply fort for Wall, with best-preserved granaries in Roman Britain. Site museum. *Corstopitum*.

*Chesters, Northumberland (NY 9170) March–April 9–5, Sun. 2–4.30; May–Sept 9–5.30, Sun 2–5; Oct–Feb 9.30–4, Sun 2–4. On the B6318 at Chollerford. Well-preserved fort, with outstanding outlying bath building and bridge abutment (approached from opposite side of river). *Cilurnum*. (See p 80)

*Housesteads, Northumberland (NY 7968) **S Sm** Path from the B6318, signposted. Best-preserved Roman fort in Britain, with one of finest stretches of Hadrian's Wall running from it. *Vercovicium*. (See p 80)

*Chesterholm, Northumberland (NY 7764) April 9.30–5, May–Sept 9.30–

6.30, Oct–March 10.30–3.30 for the new excavations. Fort **A** Signposted from B8316. Supply fort for Hadrian's Wall and civil settlement. Reconstructions of Wall, etc. Site museum. *Vindolanda.* (See p 15)

Birdoswald, Cumbria (NY 6166) **A On the B6318. Well-preserved walls and gates of fort. *Camboglanna.* (See p 74)

**Brunton turret, Northumberland (NY 9269) Off the A6079. Best-preserved turret on the Wall.

Limestone Corner, Northumberland (NY 8771) On B6318. Outstanding rock-cut section of ditch.

Carrawburgh, Temple of Mithras, Northumberland (NY 8571) **A On the B6318, about 1m beyond Limestone Corner. Slight remains of Roman fort and adjacent restored foundations of temple.

Poltross Burn, Northumberland (NY 6366) **A On B6318. Best preserved milecastle on Wall. (See p 82)

Willowford, Northumberland (NY 6266) **A Outstanding section of Wall on B6318, not far from Poltross Burn. Two turrets and bridge abutment with ruined mill.

The Antonine Wall

Rough Castle, Stirlingshire (NS 8479) **A 1½m E of Bonnybridge. B816 and side road. Earth rampart and ditches of fort; Lilia to N. (See p 82)

Watling Lodge, Stirlingshire (NS 8679) **A Best-preserved section of Antonine Wall and ditch, 1½m w of centre of Falkirk on B816.

Seabegs Wood, Stirlingshire (NS 8179) **A 1¼m sw of Bonnybridge, on B816. Well-preserved section of rampart and ditch.

Well-preserved sites not in State care

Fishbourne, Sussex (SU 8404) March, April, Oct 10–4; May–Sept 10–7; week-ends only Nov; closed Dec–Feb, 1½m w of Chichester, on A27 to Portsmouth. Very impressive villa with many amenities. (See p 36)

Bignor, Sussex (SU 9814) March–Oct 10–6.30; closed Mondays except in August; open Bank Holidays. Villa with very fine mosaics, 14m from Chichester on A285 and side road. Closed Nov–1 March

Silchester, Hants (SU 6462) Map essential to find it. Impressive town walls and earthworks, not built over. *Calleva Atrebatum*.

Brading, Isle of Wight (SZ 6086) May–Sept 9.30–6, Sun 3–6, or by arrangement with custodian. 1½m sw of Brading. Very impressive mosaics at this villa.

Chedworth, Glos (SP 0513) Closed Mon—except Bank Holidays, 1–15 Oct and throughout Jan. Opening hours 10–1, 2–7—or dusk if earlier. Best-preserved villa in Britain. Museum, mosaics. (See p 39)

St Albans, Herts (TL 1307) Verulamium museum, open weekdays April–Oct 10–5.30; Nov–March 10–4, Sun 2–4. Theatre, open every day from 10 until dusk. About one-third of 200-acre town excavated. *Verulamium*. (See p 55)

Baginton, the Lunt, Warwicks (SP 344752) Opening times under review. 2m s of Coventry. Impressive reconstruction of timber fort. (See p 64)

Cardiff Castle, South Glamorgan (ST 1876) Striking reconstruction of SE and part of s walls of fort. National Museum of Wales nearby.

SITES IN TOWNS

Canterbury, Kent (TR 1457) Many scattered fragments of town of *Durovernum Cantiacorum*. Finds in Royal Museum, High Street. Open weekdays 9.30–5.30.

Dorchester, Dorset (SY 6990) Scattered remains of *Durnovaria*. Town house, amphitheatre, aqueduct. Finds in Dorset County Museum, High West Street. Open Mon–Sat 10–5, closed Mon and Sat 1–2.

Exeter, Devon (SX 9192) Fragments of wall of *Isca Dumnoniorum*. Archaeological Museum, Northern Hay Gardens. Open 10–5.30 Mon–Sat.

Cirencester, Glos (so 0201) Scattered remains of *Corinium Dobunnorum*, second largest town in Roman Britain. Amphitheatre, section of defences. Outstanding Corinium Museum. Open weekdays 10–4.30 Oct to April; 10–5.30 May–Sept. Closed 1–2. Open Sun. 2–5.30 June Aug only. (See p 53)

Colchester, Essex (TL 9925) Colonia of *Camulodunum*. Scattered remains include town wall, Balkerne Gate, foundation of Temple of Claudius. Good museum in Castle, open weekdays 10–5. (See p 48)

Lincoln, Lincs (SK 9771) Colonia of *Lindum*. Remains include famous Newport Arch, still in use, and other gates of colonia, as well as sections of wall, etc. Finds in County Museum, Broadgate Street. Open weekdays 10–5.30, Sun 2–5.30

Leicester, Leics (SK 5804) Town of *Ratae Coritanorum*. Main remains are on Jewry Wall site, with its 30ft high mass of masonry. Adjacent site museum, both open weekdays 10.30–7, Sat from 9.30 and Sun 2–5.

Chester, Cheshire (SJ 4066) Roman fortress of Deva. Various fragments, including sections of fourth-century fort walls crowned by later town walls. Amphitheatre* **A** Important collection of finds in Grosvenor Museum. (See p 61)

London Numerous scattered remains, including reconstructed foundations of Temple of Mithras and sections of wall in grounds of Tower of London.

OTHER VISIBLE REMAINS IN ROMAN BRITAIN

Site	Grid Reference	Type of Site	County
Ackling Dyke	su 0116	Linear earthwork	Dorset
Aldborough	se 4066	Town	Yorks
Ambleside	NY 3703	Fort	Cumbria
Ancaster	SK 9843	Town	Lincs
Ardoch	NN 8309	Fort	Perth
Bartlow	TL 5844	Burial mounds	Essex
Binchester	NZ 2131	Fort	Co Durham
Birdhope	NY 8298	Camp	Northumb
Birrens	NY 2175	Fort	Dumfries

Site	Grid Reference	Type of Site	County
Bitterne	SU 4313	Fort	Hants
Black Carts	NY 8871	Wall	Northumb
Blackstone Edge	SD 9616	Road	Lancs
Bowes	NY 9913	Fort	Yorks
Brough	NY 7914	Fort	Cumbria
Brougham	NY 5328	Fort	Cumbria
Burnswark	NY 1878	Siegeworks	Dumfries
Caer Gai	SH 8731	Fort	Gwynedd
Caer Gybi	SH 2482	Fort	Gwynedd
Caerhun	SH 8731	Fort	Gwynedd
Caer Leb	SH 4767	Native site	Gwynedd
Caister-on-Sea	TG 5212	Town	Norfolk
Caistor	TA 1101	Town	Lincs
Caistor St Edmund	TG 2303	Town	Norfolk
Carlisle	NY 3955	Fort	Cumbria
Castell Collen	SO 0562	Fort	Powys
Castle Greg	NT 0459	Fortlet	Midlothian
Chew Green	NT 7808	Camps	Northumb
Clyro	SO 2243	Fort	Hereford
Cramond	NT 1977	Fort	Midlothian
Din Lligwy	SH 4986	Native site	Gwynedd
Denton Hall	NZ 1965	Wall	Northumb
Dolaucothi	SN 6640	Mine	Dyfed
Dover	TR 3141	Fort	Kent
Ebchester	NZ 1055	Fort	Northumb
Gask Ridge	NN 9118	Signal station	Perth
Gelligaer	ST 1397	Fort	Glamorgan
Gloucester	SO 8318	Fort	Glos
Grassington	SE 0065	Fields	Yorks
Great Casterton	TF 0009	Town	Leics
Greatchesters	NY 7066	Fort	Northumb
Great Witcombe	SO 8914	Villa	Glos
Greta Bridge	NZ 0813	Fort	Yorks
Halton	NY 9968	Fort	Northumb
Heddon	NZ 1366	Wall	Northumb
High Rochester	NY 8398	Fort	Northumb
Hod Hill	ST 8510	Fort	Dorset
Horncastle	TF 2569	Town	Lincs

Site	Grid Reference	Type of Site	County
Ilkley	SE 1148	Fort	Yorks
Inchtuthil	NO 1239	Fortress	Perth
Jordon Hill	SY 6982	Temple	Dorset
Keston	TQ 4163	Burial site	Kent
Keynsham	ST 6469	Villa	Avon
King's Weston	ST 5377	Villa	Avon
Kirkbuddo	NO 4944	Camp	Angus
Lanchester	NZ 1546	Fort	Co Durham
Latimer	SU 9998	Villa	Bucks
Lydney	SO 6102	Temple	Glos
Lympne	TR 1134	Fort	Kent
Lyne	NT 1840	Fort	Peebles
Malton	SE 7971	Fort	Yorks
Martinhoe	SS 6649	Fortlet	Devon
Maryport	NY 0337	Fort	Cumbria
Mersea Island	TM 0214	Tomb	Essex
Middleton	SD 6285	Milestone	Cumbria
Neath	SS 7497	Fort	Glamorgan
New Kilpatrick	NS 5572	Wall	Dunbarton
Newport	SZ 5088	Villa	IOW
Normandykes	NO 8399	Camp	Aberdeen
North Leigh	SP 3915	Villa	Oxon
Old Burrow	SS 7849	Fortlet	Devon
Piercebridge	NZ 2115	Fort	Co Durham
Raedykes	NO 8490	Camp	Kincardine
Ravenglass	SD 0895	Fort	Cumbria
Reculver	TR 2269	Fort	Kent
Rey Cross	NY 9012	Camp	Yorks
Ribchester	SD 6535	Fort	Lancs
Risingham	NY 8986	Fort	Northumb
Rudchester	NZ 1167	Fort	Northumb
Scarborough	TA 0589	Signal station	Yorks
Sea Mills	ST 5575	Settlement	Avon
Soldier's Ring	SU 0817	Native ranch	Wilts
South Shields	NZ 3667	Fort	Tyne-and-Wear
Stevenage	TL 2323	Burial mounds	Herts
Stone-by-Faversham	TQ 9961	Burial site	Kent

Site	Grid Reference	Type of Site	County
Swine Hill	NY 9082	Camp	Northumb
Temple Sowerby	NY 6226	Milestone	Cumbria
Thornborough	SP 7333	Burial mounds	Bucks
Tomen-y-Mur	SH 7038	Fort	Gwynedd
Waterbeach	TL 4867	Linear earthwork	Cambs
Wheeldale Moor	SE 8097	Road	Yorks
Whitley Castle	NY 6948	Fort	Cumbria
Woden Law	NT 7612	Siegeworks	Roxburgh
Y Pigwyn	SN 8231	Fort	Powys

SOME MUSEUMS WITH ROMAN COLLECTIONS

Aylesbury
Bangor
Barnard Castle
Bath
Bedford
Birmingham: City Museum
Bradford: City Art Gallery and Museum
Brecon
Bristol City Museum
Bury St Edmund's: Moyse's Hall
Buxton
Cambridge Museum of Archaeology & Ethnology
Canterbury: Royal Museum
Cardiff: National Museum of Wales
Carlisle
Carmarthen
Chelmsford
Chester: Grosvenor Museum
Chichester
Cirencester: Corinium Museum
Colchester: Castle Museum
Devizes
Doncaster
Dorchester: Dorset County Museum
Dover
Dumfries Museum
Edinburgh: National Museum of Antiquities
Exeter: Rougemont House Museum
Falkirk
Folkestone
Glasgow: Hunterian Museum
Gloucester: City Museum
Hereford: City Museum
Huddersfield: Tolson Memorial Museum
Hull: Transport & Archaeology Museum
Ilkley
Ipswich
Kidderminster
Lancaster
Leeds City Museum
Leicester: Jewry Wall Museum
Lincoln: City Museum
London: British Museum, London Museum

Maidstone
Malton
Manchester: City Art Gallery
Newark
Newbury
Newcastle: Museum of Anti-
quities
Northampton
Norwich Castle Museum
Oxford: Ashmolean Museum
Peterborough
Reading Museum & Art Gallery
Rochester
St Albans: Verulamium Museum
Saffron Walden

Salisbury
Scunthorpe
Sheffield: City Museum
Shrewsbury: Rowley's House
Museum
Southampton: God's Tower
House Museum
Sunderland
Taunton
Warwick
Winchester: City Museum
Worcester: City Museum
Yeovil
York: Yorkshire Museum

Acknowledgements

I should like to thank my husband Lloyd for his constant help and encouragement, and John Eames, who taught me Classical Archaeology at Liverpool University and Caroline Washbourn who helped with the line drawings.

Index

Numbers in italic type refer to plate pages.

STANBOROUGH SCHOOL
WELWYN GARDEN CITY